OVERTAXED!
Your Guide to Honest Property Tax Reductions
by Understanding and Effectively Protesting Your Assessment

by
Ed C. Tomlinson

Diamond Publications

5440 Ward Road, Suite 110
Arvada, CO 80002

ISBN 0-9626776-3-9

LCCN 90-086128

The following trademark appears throughout this book: Realtor.

DEDICATION

To my wife, Joan, who allowed me to spend countless time, effort, and financial resources on this project, supporting and believing in me every step of the way.

To the Tomlinson family:

TODAY
YESTERDAY
TOMORROW

ACKNOWLEDGEMENTS

Many people and organizations contributed their thought, time, and talent to this book.

Several members of the media merit special attention. Their messages enabled me to help thousands of property owners throughout Colorado. Mary Kay Conner, editor of the Arvada Sentinel newspaper, gave me confidence in my initial work in the property tax system by helping me realize that the public need for information and help with property tax assessments was real, and not imagined. David Lewis of the Rocky Mountain News provided even more confidence through his sincere compliments on the 1988 issue of my tax guide. His article proved to be instrumental in the acceptance and success of the guide.

I also thank the dozens of radio stations, magazines, and newspapers around the state—including The Rocky Mountain News and The Denver Post—whose coverage has served to help the people of Colorado. In particular, I thank John Rebchook of the Rocky Mountain News.

The KOA radio staff, including Jerry Bell, Tom Martino, and Arzella Dirksen, helped make my work a news item in 1988 and 1989. The news and editorial staffs at KCNC-TV, KMGH-TV, and KWGN-TV provided additional coverage, serving to bolster my confidence and spread the word to even more Coloradoans.

On the legislative front, Ted Strickland and Paul Schauer displayed a sincere interest in my work and the issues raised. The Colorado State Legislative Council reprinted and distributed over 100 copies of my prior guides and invited me to address the Senate and House Interim Tax Committee on recommendations for the property tax system. Also, Jack O'Donnell, Mary Huddleston, and the staff at the State Division of Property Taxation has provided invaluable assistance, easy accessibility, unbiased attitudes, and a wealth of knowledge on any assessment topic. They also provided a valuable review of this manuscript for accuracy.

Finally, I acknowledge the thousands of people who have sought help from me. Their appreciation and feedback has let me know that one person can make a difference. Thank you.

FOREWORD

Most people complain about taxes, but few people do anything about them. This concise and straightforward book will help you to get a fair appraisal by assessors and do something about the taxes levied on your property.

Often, individuals find the appraisal process used for tax assessment to be complex and confusing. It is of value to all of us to know how property value is determined for tax purposes and what we can do to make sure that the processes are properly followed.

By knowing the system and the procedures used to operate it, one is more successful in making it work. Every person concerned about property taxes should take the time to become acquainted with the processes and techniques used in this book, be it on a professional basis or for personal concern. Many people feel that protesting taxes is just for the commercial property owner, but the process is available and open to every property owner. But one has to do something about it.

That is where this book is very helpful. What appears to many as a morass of technicalities and legalities is reduced to an effective, straightforward system by the author. In addition, effective strategies to work with assessors are addressed.

Taking the time to read this book and then utilizing the information will be well worth the time and effort that a person invests. The author has done the hard work to reduce the pain and trauma of other people learning something on their own.

Too often people become emotional about their taxes. Instead they should find out about the system and how it works. The author helps the reader work through the system so that they can objectively develop a response to their taxes.

Overtaxed!—Your Guide to Honest Property Tax Reductions by Understanding and Effectively Protesting Your Assessment will help you better understand local government's claim on property tax as a source of revenue. With that understanding, not only will you be making sure that you are taxed fairly, but you will become more appreciative of the services you receive from your local government.

Gordon E. Von Stroh, Ph.D.   University of Denver

TABLE OF CONTENTS

PREFACE

Thank you for your interest in my work in the Colorado property tax assessment system. Because I am not personally able to assist the thousands of property owners who have requested my help, I have written this book to help you evaluate your own tax assessment position.

Colorado property owners protested over 175,000 assessments in 1989 alone (see Appendix A). Their actions resulted in tens of millions of dollars in proper appraisal reductions and honest refunds of over $27 million in back taxes (see Appendices B and C). Understanding how the state's property tax assessment system works will give you the opportunity to intelligently review your property's valuation for fairness and accuracy. Tens of thousands of residential and commercial property owners throughout the state have reduced their taxes substantially by identifying errors in the valuations made by the county assessors. Now you have the chance to do the same.

I commend you on your decision to take responsibility for your property taxes. Since the law currently requires county assessors to update property appraisals every other year (and starting in 1993, every year), it is in your best interest to find out what your role is in the tax assessment system. Reviewing your tax position is not difficult or expensive, but it does require some time and patience. I assure you, however, that your efforts will pay off in tax reductions and peace of mind.

INTRODUCTION

This book is designed for busy people who want to understand and learn how to review and lower property tax assessments efficiently and effectively. This includes property owners, Realtors, property managers, attorneys, appraisers, legislators and those corporate employees trusted to know these things. The process is not that hard, and does not take much money, if you invest a little time to learn about the property tax system and your role in it. The book is meant to be read from beginning to end. Once you have read it entirely, you can easily refer to specific sections.

Over $2 billion is collected in property taxes each year in Colorado, the largest collection of taxes in the state outside of federal income taxes (see Appendix D). The property tax system includes $162 billion of real estate value (see Appendix E) and over 2 million individual properties. In such a large system, mistakes are bound to be made—mistakes which can cost you a bundle in taxes. But these mistakes won't correct themselves. Under Colorado law, you have the right to file a protest. It's simple: if you don't file a protest, and your assessment is inaccurate, you will end up paying more than you should. The burden of proof is on you.

The problem is that many property owners just look at their property tax bills each year and pay them, assuming they can't do much about them. On the other hand, owners of commercial, industrial and apartment buildings routinely fight to lower their property tax assessments. The average homeowner (the one who has the best chance to win a protest) just pays the bill and lets the issue pass.

But most of us really can't afford to ignore our property tax bills. Look at reviewing your tax position and protesting as part of maintaining your home. If you are like most people, real estate is the biggest investment in your life. You take pride in your property and don't hesitate to repair your property when essential maintenance is required. That's the way you should perceive your property tax assessment—you have to be ready to step in to repair your assessment when a correction is required.

You can save anywhere from a few dollars to hundreds of thousands of dollars if you are successful in appealing your assessment. Whether you are successful or not depends on how well you prepare and present your case, and how well (or how poorly) your local assessor handles his/her job. I have learned that almost everyone can present a credible protest with the proper background material and suggestions (which this book offers you).

Property taxes in Colorado are determined in large part through an appraisal system administered by county assessors. Assessors and their staff members are people just like you and me. Each assessor is different. When working with them, most will be very helpful and a few will be defensive.

This book will prepare you, the property owner, for any situation that may arise while working with assessors. Be assured, however, that most assessors will cooperate fully with you.

The book can be used very effectively for both residential and commercial properties. Residential properties are defined by assessors as houses, mobile homes, duplexes, and *apartment buildings*.

Large commercial property owners may wish to employ the services of tax agents for assistance or delegate the job to an in-house tax staff. Commercial tax agents generally retain about 50 percent (negotiable) of any tax savings obtained as their fee. For information on specific companies, refer to metropolitan Yellow Pages listings under "Taxes—Consultants & Representatives" (see Appendix F).

If you need information on agricultural properties, large land holdings, or personal property, contact the State Division of Property Taxation at (303) 866-2371. You can purchase a copy of the rules and regulations for these types of properties from the Division.

Chapter 1

WHY BOTHER?

You may be wondering if it's worth your time not only to read this book, but to review your tax position. To that end, I encourage you to read, or reread, the Introduction, along with the following: excuses property owners use to avoid taking a look at their tax positions—and the reasons those excuses just won't stand up!

You can't fight city hall. Yes you can! Property owners received over $27 million in 1989 just in cash refunds as a result of protesting. That doesn't include the estimated $30 million dollars in property tax reductions—just *refunds* from prior-year mistakes (see Appendix G). In 1989, the average refund was $1,675.

I'm afraid that if I bring my taxes to the attention of the assessor, he/she will find some other problems and raise my assessment. The fact of the matter is that this just doesn't happen. If your protest is unsuccessful, your assessment will remain the same in almost all cases. State review boards can not use an individual's appeal hearings as a device to raise his/her (or a neighbor's) assessment.

It wouldn't make sense for me to file a protest, because the assessor's estimate of my home's market value is a lot less than I think it's really worth. Never make assumptions about the assessor's appraisal. Do your homework before making any conclusions. It is very important to understand that assessors do not talk about a property's current market value. They are only concerned with a value for tax purposes—and that value generally is lower than the property's fair market value. In fact, one of the best ways to judge the accuracy of your appraisal is to compare it to assessor's appraisals on other similar properties.

I'd be too nervous if I had to go through an appeal hearing. Remember that it is your legal right to protest your assessment. And it is your responsibility to initiate the process to find and correct errors. Take some time and do some research—with a little background information, your confidence will increase greatly. Keep in mind that property owners just like you filed protests on 175,000 properties in 1989!

Appealing my property tax assessment is too complicated and takes too much time. Wouldn't it be worth it to spend a few hours for the chance of saving several hundred dollars? Most of us don't make nearly that much on an hourly basis—It seems like a good investment of time to me.

Also, remember that the process is easier than it sounds. You really don't have to be an attorney to put together an effective property tax protest.

Chapter 2

HOW YOUR PROPERTY TAXES ARE DETERMINED

Property taxes are based on a combination of the assessor's appraisal of your property, the current assessment rate, and your local area's mill levies. Assessment rates, which I will explain later in this chapter, are set by law. Mill levies are determined by your local taxing authorities. The only real variable in the equation is the appraisal.

The Appraisal

The appraisal is the dollar value assigned to your property by your county's assessor. It is *not* your property's current fair market value. Take care never to rely on the assessor's appraisal in any buying or selling decisions. The assessor has probably never seen your property (nor any comparable properties). Beyond that, assessors' information about the property can be subject to widespread error.

Case in point: Last year, a couple sold their home to their son and daughter-in-law at a price based on the assessor's value of the home. Because the assessment was flawed, the son and daughter-in-law paid $20,000 more than the property was worth. Both parties acted in good faith, but relied on an assessor's appraisal.

It is also important for you to understand that the appraisal the assessor makes on your home or property is, by definition, different than the appraisals done by insurance companies, banks, or Realtors. *Again, the assessor's value is not used for any purpose other than property tax determination.*

For example, the insurance appraisal which estimates how much it would take to replace your property in event of fire is almost always much higher than what a buyer would pay for your house. Likewise, a bank's appraisal for a second mortgage or equity loan is intended for collateral purposes and is not meant to determine what your property is worth to a buyer. It, too, would generally be higher than what a buyer would pay for your property.

Since assessors have control over the appraisal, and only the appraisal, any review or protest of your tax position must focus on the appraisal, not your actual taxes. Your property's appraisal is the only factor in the tax determination process over which you have direct control. The rest of this book, therefore, will concentrate on the accuracy of the assessor's appraisal of your property.

"Appraisal" is used interchangeably with "valuation," "total value," "actual value," and, most often, with "total actual value."

Three Approaches to Determining Appraisals

To determine your property's appraisal, assessors may use a market approach, cost approach, or income approach, depending on the type of property you own.

1. Market approach
   The market approach involves identifying comparable sales for your property. It is almost always the best approach for home owners and assessors to use in appraising residential properties. It is based on two factors:
   — what the assessor knows about your property, as recorded on a property appraisal card on file at his/her office
   — adjusted sales prices of properties similar to yours, from transactions occurring in the base period (which will be explained in Chapter 7).

2. Cost approach

This approach involves determining the exact worth of every piece of a building (as listed on the appraisal card): today's cost (replacement cost of the building, including land improvements such as parking lots and concrete walkways) less depreciation. Land value is then determined and added to the cost.

While appropriate under certain limited circumstances (such as for brand-new structures), it is not as accurate as the market approach. One reason for this is because of the difficulty in determining the exact amount of depreciation which has occurred. This approach usually results in higher appraisals than do the market and income approaches, and it is impossible to prove or disprove.

Several services provide cost information to assessors to help them determine today's costs. The most commonly used of these is the Marshall & Swift set of manuals. Other state-approved reference books are the Boeckh's and R.S. Means manuals (available in local libraries). Most assessors start with the information provided by Marshall & Swift and then alter it to suit their own purposes through computer-assisted appraisal programs. Once altered, it is difficult to identify the factors used in the calculation.

Once current costs have been determined, depreciation is calculated. Depreciation adjustments can be classified into three categories:

a. *physical deterioration*—the natural wearing out of the structure, creating a reduced value. Physical deterioration can be *curable* or *incurable*.

Curable deterioration is deterioration which can be fixed, and is economically advantageous to fix. Examples include exterior repainting and reroofing. Incurable deterioration is deterioration for which the costs of repair, maintenance, or modernization outweigh the advantages of making the repair.

b. *functional obsolescence*—awkward floor plans (especially after room additions) which make properties less

valuable. Costs to be incurred to correct such deficien-
cies are included as additional depreciation. Functional
obsolescence may be curable or incurable.

c. *economic obsolescence*—caused by a number of
factors under which you have no control. This type of
depreciation applies primarily to apartments, commercial and industrial property. Examples include deterio-
rating economic conditions in the neighborhood,
location of the property on a once-busy, now-quiet
street, and cases in which rents can not cover the
operating expenses of a building.

Many assessors implement a "neighborhood adjustment"
(NHAJ) factor in the cost and market approaches. The
adjustment is a monetary amount which some assessors add
to or subtract from the property's appraisal to bring the two
approaches' (cost and market) figures in line with each other.
This "neighborhood adjustment," generally undetected by the
property owner, is often used as a technique by the assessor
to defend his/her position. Its correct purpose is to adjust the
difference in value of one similar neighborhood to another.

3. Income approach
   The income approach involves proving a property's
valuation through its net income and expenses. While this
approach is not allowed for use on residential properties,
it often is the commercial property owners' best chance
to correct an appraisal. It is the most accurate method to
use. Property value is equal to:

$$\frac{\text{(actual gross income minus operating expenses)}}{\text{capitalization rate}}$$

Expenses exclude goodwill, principal reduction, and
interest. The property is appraised by the assessor as
though it was free and clear. The capitalization, or "cap"
rate, is used to determine the rate of return on cash
invested. For example, if you paid $100,000 cash for a
property and wanted a $10,000 (10 percent) annual return,
your cap rate would be 10. The cap rate varies according
to the risk you are taking, and is usually 11-14 percent.

To help determine the correct rate, contact one of the following:

— Your assessor. Make sure you know how he/she arrived at the rate.
— A commercial real estate appraiser (see Appendix H) or Realtor
— Commercial Building Owners and Managers Association (B.O.M.A.) at (303) 820-2662

Assessment

The assessment amount is a percentage of the assessor's appraisal on your property. It is determined by multiplying the assessment rate, set by state law, by the assessor's appraisal value of your property.

The current residential assessment rate is 14.34 percent. The rate for commercial property (as well as vacant residential lots) is firm at 29 percent. As the residential rates are subject to slight changes, you may want to call the State Division of Property Taxation at (303) 866-2371 for verification.

Suppose an assessor appraises a residential property at $100,000. The assessment amount of the property would be $14,340 ($100,000 x .1434). If a commercial property is appraised at $100,000, its assessment would be $29,000 ($100,000 x .29).

Property Tax Calculation

Once the assessment is calculated, it is multiplied by the mill levy to determine your actual tax bill. The taxing districts in which your property is located determine the number of taxing entities that go into your mill levy. There are about 2,000 different districts in the state. You may have 6-12 districts: one for police, one for fire, one for schools, etc.

Using the above example, let's say that the total mill levy for all your taxing districts is 71. Since 1 mill is equal to 1/10 of 1 cent (.001), that is $.071. The taxes owed, therefore, on the $100,000 residential property would be $14,340 x .071, or $1,081.14. The taxes owed on the $100,000 commercial property would be $29,000 x .071, or $2,059.

As you can see, owners of commercial/industrial property (and vacant residential lots) are paying almost twice the tax a similarly valued residential property owner is paying. This is no accident: State law currently requires non-residential property owners to pay 55 percent of the total property tax burden. When you read or hear that the residential assessment rate is being changed, it means that the rate, or percent, discussed above is being modified to ensure that the current law is being enforced.

Many assessors also have a brochure explaining the assessment system. Ask for it.

Reappraisal

Current state law requires counties to *assess* all properties (multiply the appraisal value by the assessment rate) every January 1, and to *reappraise* properties (reevaluate property values) every two years.

This year's reappraisal, the 1991 reappraisal, carries an official appraisal date of June 30, 1990. Appraisals are actually based on adjusted sale prices of properties sold between January 1, 1989 and June 30, 1990 (in most counties), *adjusted* to June 30, 1990, prices. The tax bill you receive next January will be based on the current (1991) reappraisal value, the assessment rate, the condition of your property on January 1, and current mill levies.

Chapter 3

WHY YOUR PROPERTY TAX BILL MAY BE INCORRECT

Mass Appraisal Method

Property values are determined by a Mass Appraisal Method used by all county assessors in Colorado. Using a computerized process, assessors appraise over two million properties a year. While the system results in fairly accurate overall audit results, some assessors recognize that it also results in many properties being appraised higher than they should be.

That is exactly why the protest system was developed: to correct individual property errors. In fact, my research into the assessment practices of 11 major Colorado counties suggests that assessors (albeit inadvertently) overvalue one-third of all residential properties, some as much as 50 percent or more. Many assessors will admit this confidentially. Overvaluation of commercial properties is even more prevalent.

To prove this, one can review the assessor's sales ratio analysis report. The report, a listing of property sales in the base period (see Chapter 7), compares the assessor's appraisals of properties with the prices for which those properties sold. The report is an excellent reflection of the overall accuracy of property appraisals in the county.

Frequently Asked Questions

Reappraisals create many questions for property owners. Some of the most frequently asked are addressed below.

Question: The assessor's 1991 appraisal of my property is higher than the 1989 appraisal amount. How could that have happened when property values fell between those years?

Answer: One of three things may have happened.
  1. The assessor may have believed property values in your area increased, based on the comparables he/she reviewed.
  2. The assessor may have made an error. In many counties, foreclosures were not taken into consideration, thereby creating artificially high value bases. Also, the assessor may not have used comparables which were appropriate for your property. And in some counties, a few assessors may have plugged arbitrary factors into the formula due to time or staffing restrictions.
  3. Your prior appraisal may have been too low.

Question: Is it possible for land and improvement valuations to go up and down in different directions?

Answer: Yes. Many property owners found this situation during prior reappraisals. Many assessors reappraise land and improvements (buildings, for example) separately, and then add the two values together to arrive at one appraisal amount. The formulas used in determining the separate amounts were shown to be inconsistent in many cases during prior reappraisals.

Question: My appraisal decreased, but could my taxes still go up?

Answer: Yes, for several reasons. The assessor's appraisal of your property may fall slightly, but not as much as the appraisals of other properties in your county. Therefore, you would be paying a larger proportion of the total property tax bill than before. For example, your valuation might drop two percent, but the overall county's could drop six percent. This may be especially true this year for commercial properties.

Another possibility is that mill levies may have increased enough to offset the advantage resulting from a reduced appraisal. Also, if you live in a rural county, there is the possibility of mill levy increases to make up for losses incurred from other tax bases which generate income for the county. If you live in a county with many town-homes, condominiums, or apartment buildings, your situation may be affected by these properties. These types of properties generally fell in value more than single-family homes did. But the *entire* residential property base of the county is responsible for the residential share of taxes. Subsequently, owners of single-family homes could end up paying a proportionately higher share of the total tax burden.

For example, the values of single-family homes could fall 10 percent, but the value of apartment and condominium buildings in the same county may have dropped 40 percent.

Chapter 4

REVIEWING YOUR APPRAISAL CARD

The Appraisal Card

The appraisal card is an extremely important piece of information affecting your appraisal. Data about your property is recorded on the card (which may actually be a computer printout of one or more pages) at your county assessor's office. Assessors base their appraisals on this data, which they call "inventory." If it is wrong or incomplete, your appraisal (and resulting tax bill) will be incorrect. As many as 70 percent of these cards contain errors. It is your responsibility to review your property's appraisal card for accuracy. Some assessors send this information out to you every reappraisal year (i.e., every other year).

When to Review Your Appraisal Card

You can review the card any time of the year, but assessors are only *required* to make reductions in valuation resulting from appraisal card errors through June 1. Reductions noted after that date, and up until early December (when assessors turn the assessment data over to the county treasurer for billing purposes), might be reflected in next January's tax bill; it is at the assessor's option. If you do review your card and make corrections, you may need to review it again in 1993, when the next reappraisal is done, because corrections in some counties may not be recorded permanently.

How to Obtain a Copy of Your Appraisal Card

Contact your county assessor's office by phone, mail, or in person (see Appendix I), and request a *complete* copy of your appraisal card data.

Reviewing Your Appraisal Card for Accuracy

The more thorough you are in reviewing your appraisal card data, the more comfortable you will be in understanding the assessment system. Take time to understand it fully.

Accurate data—You'll find information on size, style, and condition of your home, number of bedrooms and baths, lot size, square footage, etc. When verifying square footage, be sure to measure around the exterior of the property. Measure a basement or garage separately. If you need assistance, use your survey, call a neighbor, an appraiser (see Appendix H), or a local Realtor.

Commercial property owners can collect additional data, such as warehouse ceiling heights, etc. Apartment building owners should also check the card for the correct number of apartments in the building, number of bedrooms in each apartment, etc.

Proper notation of additions and improvements to the property—Several years ago, some assessors may have added the value of an addition to the appraisal card data, but then not have deleted the value of the old, torn-down structure it replaced. For instance, a former owner may have converted an attached one-car garage into a family room. While the assessor may have noted the room addition on the card, he/she may not have removed the garage's value from the card. Some assessors may even add a finished basement to your appraisal card automatically after a property reaches 10 years of age, because they realize many property owners finish their basements without pulling a building permit.

Existing property condition—Make sure that the proper condition of all structures on your property is noted. In one recent case, a property owner had a second house on the back of his property. The assessor did not know, however, that the house had been abandoned years ago, and had no heat, electricity, or water. By proving that the building should be appraised as a large storage shed rather than a home, the owner reduced his property appraisal by over $35,000 (along with another $35,000 reduction for the poor condition of his main house), resulting in a tax reduction of over $700 per year.

Property condition as of January 1—Think about the condition your property was in on January 1. Even though this year's assessment is generally based on property values between January 1, 1989, and June 30, 1990, changes occurring in property condition after that time period and before January 1 of this year can affect your appraisal. Specifically, during the last year, was your property subject to fire, flood, hail, wind, tenant damage, structural damage, uncorrected curable depreciation, etc.—and not returned to its original condition by January 1? If so, ask that the change in valuation be noted on your card.

Other adverse changes affecting property—During the last year, did your next-door neighbor erect a commercial building next to your home, reducing its value? Did the city change policy and no longer allow you to park on your street? Was your street changed to a one-way, creating more traffic? Has the city changed traffic flow in other ways, resulting in more people driving by your property? Have these or other changes been noted on the card?

Does your property border on a busy street? Is there a ditch running through or alongside your property? Is your property located next to a railroad track? Does your basement get wet every few rainstorms because of foundation problems? Is your property located in a flood plain? Have these or other changes been noted on the card?

Commercial owners, have you discovered asbestos? Has the traffic flow or pattern changed at your location?

Chapter 5

REPORT APPRAISAL CARD ERRORS

State law is clear in that every property is to be appraised individually (Colorado Revised Statutes 39-5-104 and 39-5-105(1)). It is your right and obligation to note any errors with the appraisal card data to the assessor and request an appropriate adjustment.

Report errors to the assessor

When you find mistakes with your appraisal card data, note them and bring them to the attention of your assessor for correction. Whether the errors are in your favor or the assessor's, it is in your best interest over the long term to report them. Assessors will rarely send a county appraiser to your property to confirm an error unless it is a major one. Instead, they will usually correct the error in the office. You do have the right, however, to a visit from the assessor if you believe it is warranted.

If the assessor agrees with you about the errors, the County Commissioners, who have final responsibility for the decision, will usually just approve the correction. If the assessor is in disagreement with your request, you will be notified of a hearing (meeting) with the commissioners (or their representatives). In some years, up to 95 percent of these reductions are granted, equating to tens of millions of dollars. If, however, you are not totally satisfied with the commissioners' decision, you may carry your appeal further (see Chapter 12, Board of Assessment Appeals).

File for a tax refund

If substantial errors are found on your appraisal card, consider filing for a tax refund with the one-page "Petition for Abatement or Refund of Taxes" form (see Appendix J) obtained from your assessor, County Clerk and Recorder's Office, or County Treasurer. Your assessor is supposed to help you complete it. Be aware that each county handles abatements on a different time schedule. Processing can take anywhere from a few weeks to many months.

You can file for a refund of back taxes for up to two years if you have owned the property during that time and the error was reflected in your appraisal. Although you can file until December 31, it is best not to delay if this situation applies to you.

Because different counties have different interpretations of the time limitations for refunds, call the State Division of Property Taxation at (303) 866-2371 for clarification. Note that if your county wishes to refund only one year's back taxes, but the state's position is different, you may appeal the commissioners' decision to the State Board of Assessment Appeals (See Chapter 12).

Chapter 6

REVIEWING THE ASSESSOR'S APPRAISAL NOTICE OF VALUE

Receipt of Appraisal Notice

In early May of 1991, you should have received a notice of value (appraisal) for the 1991 reappraisal. If you do not have this notice, contact your county assessor today to find out the assessor's current value ("Total Actual Value") of your property. You may not have received the notice for one of three reasons:

1. You were not the property's owner of record in April, 1991.
2. The assessor has an inaccurate mailing address.
3. Your valuation did not change.

Information Contained in Notice

The amount on the notice includes the value of land and improvements (buildings and any other structures on the property). You will also see your prior valuation on this notice. Do not use any of these figures as a basis for determining your current tax position.

A few counties will also include an estimate of next year's tax bill on the notice. Again, do not make any decisions about the accuracy of your appraisal on the basis of this estimate.

Chapter 7

COLLECT DATA

After reviewing and correcting any errors on your appraisal card, your newly adjusted appraisal value may still be inaccurate. You should collect data to determine your own appraisal position.

Determine the Base Period

Determining your property's fair value for assessment purposes involves proving its value as of June 30, 1990, generally using the January 1, 1989—June 30, 1990, time period. This is called the *base period*.

Before you go any further, call your county assessor to see if this is the base period which he/she is using for your property (See Appendix I). By law, assessors can use a more extensive base period if there were insufficient property sales during the normal time period. For example, Jefferson County is using a two-year base period. Other counties may be using a five-year base period for some types of properties.

Assessors might want to deny any protest you present if it does not coincide with his/her chosen base period, even though you have good evidence. Find out if your assessor's base period differs from the standard, and then try to work within it.

Verify Taxing Districts

Look at your tax bill or ask your assessor in which taxing districts he/she has you listed. Every property owner has separate taxing districts for various services, including fire, sewer, water, parks and recreation, etc. If you have any question on the accuracy of the districts in which the assessor has you listed, just call the district in question to verify its boundaries.

Conduct Research Through One or More Methods

You can prove the value of your property through *one or more* of the following ways:

Comparables

The comparables method may be used in any situation, and is based on the fact that sales price can generally establish the upper limit of a property's value. As such, you will need to compare your property's appraisal with sale prices of similar properties.

Obtain a List of Sales—From the Assessor

Colorado Revised Statute 39-5-121.5 *requires* assessors to make available, upon the request of a taxpayer or his/her agent, all data used by the assessor in determining the appraisal value of any property owned by that taxpayer.

Go to or call your assessor's office and ask for a printout of the sales the assessor used in determining the value on your property. Also request a copy of the calculations (market, cost, or income) the assessor used to determine your appraisal.

In all counties, assessors can identify all property sales in a neighborhood via computer files. You should also ask for a list of sales in your neighborhood which occurred during the base period. Make sure that you get the sale price, address, identification number, appraisal value, and complete appraisal card description of the comparable properties—including foreclosures. (With a property identification number or property address, you can get a copy of any property's appraisal card from your assessor.)

If you obtain a neighborhood sales list, and find that few (or no) sales occurred in your neighborhood during the base period, ask for a list of sales in neighborhoods similar to yours. If more accurate/appropriate sales are available *after* the base period, it might be acceptable to also use those.

You may also find more accurate comparable sales in areas outside your county. For example, your neighborhood may border on a similar neighborhood located in an adjoining county. Commercial property and apartment building owners will often need to look at sales in a larger geographic area for their specific type of property (for example, a car wash), and, in some cases, in one or more counties.

Assessors can now provide you with a printed copy of these sales rather than referring you to microfiche. You can also get a list by asking for a sales ratio analysis report of your neighborhood or county. The sales ratio analysis report is usually an abbreviated list of a property's identification number, address, sales price, and assessor's appraisal value.

By law, all assessors must generate sales ratio reports. In some cases, you may be charged a small fee (generally not over $1.25/page, except in Arapahoe County, where rates are often 5-10 times higher than the norm).

Be sure you understand the assessor's information. You will find unfamiliar codes and abbreviations on the appraisal card, sales ratio analysis report, and other sales data reports. Do not be afraid to ask—and ask again—for assistance and explanations on anything you do not understand.

Should your assessor refuse to give you information on comparables, remind him/her of Colorado's public records laws guaranteeing your right to the information: First- and Second-Degree Official Misconduct (18-8-404, 18-8-405), and Abuse of Public Records (18-8-114).

Commercial and apartment building owners should contact the assessor for a complete list of sales for their *type* of property. The more specific the property description, the more need you will probably have to contact other counties' assessors for their lists. Do not hesitate to do so if you find insufficient sales in your county for your type of property.

Obtain a List of Sales—From Other Sources
Be aware that the list(s) you receive from the assessor may be incomplete. Some assessors delete sales they don't like,

such as bank, VA, and FHA foreclosures sold to the public. Many assessors never recorded any foreclosure sales prices, as they were not readily accessible. While this situation has been corrected statewide, the information will not be available in most assessors' offices until the 1993 reassessment. Additional sales (comparables) may be found through the assistance of an appraiser, Realtor, neighbors, etc.

If you are still having trouble obtaining good comparables, ask your Realtor or an appraiser for help. You can obtain names of qualified appraisers in your area through your local Board or Association of Realtors (see Appendix H). You can ask a Realtor if you may use the Multiple Listing Service (MLS) "sold" books to do your own research. Realtors in Adams, Arapahoe, Denver, Douglas, Elbert, El Paso, Jefferson, and Larimer counties can now also access all county information via the computerized Public Records System (PRS), enabling them to look up all comparable data directly from county records.

Many Front Range commercial property owners can obtain a list of land, commercial, and industrial property sales from the Roddy Reports, available through commercial brokers, at a local library, or directly through John Winslow at Dresco, (303) 691-9085. He can also create a computer-generated printout of raw data for $150-200.

Obtain Additional Information

If you want to "go the extra mile" in your research, you can then contact a Realtor and ask for a copy of the actual MLS "sold" data for those comparables you have obtained. Review them thoroughly. You may even want to call the listing agent for each property for additional information that might strengthen your case (attractive financing, property condition, etc.). If you do enlist the assistance of any Realtor, be sure to let him/her know how much you appreciate the effort.

Foreclosures

Foreclosure, for property tax purposes, is defined as the sale of a property to a new owner from a bank or other foreclosing entity.

Ask your assessor if he/she included foreclosures in the appraisal calculations on your property. In Colorado's soft (base year) real estate market, they take on added importance. Excluding foreclosures from the process will most likely result in artificially high appraisals. My informal survey of all 63 county assessors' offices in Colorado in 1989 indicated that 80 percent of them did *not* include foreclosures in the last reappraisal process. I suspect that this will be somewhat true with this reappraisal as well.

Price-per-Square-Foot

The price-per-square-foot method involves dividing the assessor's appraised value of your property by your property's square footage. For example, if the total valuation on a 1600-square-foot home is $100,000, the price per square foot would be $62.50:

$100,000 / 1600 = $62.50 (including land)

Calculate the price per square foot for your property, as well as for those properties on the lists you have obtained. At least two assessors (Denver and Jefferson County's) may do the computations for you once you have identified the comparables you wish to use. They may even supply you with a printout detailing what the assessor's exact position would be if he/she used your comparables.

For commercial properties, you can get extensive information on prices per square foot (see Appendices K, L, M, and N) from assessors, commercial Realtors, or, for Front Range commercial properties, through Dresco, (303) 691-9085, as well as the Building Owners & Managers Association (B.O.M.A.) at (303) 820-2662.

Purchase Price

If you bought your property in the base period, use this method alone or in conjunction with other methods. If your purchase represented a typical "arm's-length transaction" (i.e., you bought it on the open market and not from a family member or close business associate), the assessor's appraisal

of your property should almost always be lower than what
you paid for it.

Several items which serve to increase a property's selling
price in the marketplace are generally not considered in
assessors' appraisal calculations. The values of those items
should be deducted from the property's sale price to arrive
at a fair and correct appraisal. If the assessor's appraisal of
your home is equal to or higher than the price you paid for
it in the base period, there is a good possibility of an error.
Examples of these items include:

— Excellent financing plans, such as non-qualifying assum-
   able loans and owner-carry loans. They usually create an
   artificially high sale price compared to the price the
   property would bring if it were appraised or sold on a
   cash-offer basis.

— Cash value (depreciated value, or value in the current
   condition) of items sold with the property, including: wall-
   to-wall carpeting; free-standing household appliances;
   window coverings; personal property; water rights; mineral rights; goodwill; or fixtures owned by a tenant.

See Appendix O for information on completing the Real
Property Transfer Declaration form. A properly completed
form can reduce the valuation of a property.

Price-per-Unit

The price-per-unit method, for apartment building owners,
involves dividing the assessor's appraised value of your
property by the number of apartment units. For example, if
the total valuation on an 8-unit building is $160,000, the
price per unit would be $20,000.

$$\$160,000 \,/\, 8 = \$20,000 \text{ (including land)}$$

Calculate the price per unit for your property, as well as for
those properties on the list you have obtained.

You may need to obtain average price per unit, rental rate,
and vacancy rates (see Appendices P, Q, R, S, T, U, and V).
The more localized the information is, the better. This
information is available through several sources:

— The assessor's office—Be sure to ask *how* they obtained their data.
— Apartment and commercial property management companies (refer to local Yellow Page listings)
— Apartment Association of Metro Denver, Inc.—(303) 329-3300. The Association has available for sale surveys of metro Denver vacancy rates. The surveys are authored by Gordon E. Von Stroh, Ph.D., of the Graduate School of Business and Public Management and College of Administration at the University of Denver. The surveys are sponsored by:

Colorado Housing Finance Authority
United Banks of Colorado
Greater Denver Chamber of Commerce
U.S. Department of Housing and Urban Development
Denver Housing Authority

Other Appraisals

Use as proof any type of appraisal done on your property, preferably in the base period. A strong case can also be made for using appraisals completed after the base period. Appraisals may include (but are not limited to) appraisals from banks, the VA, or the FHA, and appraisals done for second mortgage, equity line of credit, or bond loan approvals.

Hiring an appraiser at a cost of $150-300 is usually not worth the cost for this purpose for most residential property owners. Owners of other types of properties should conduct a cost/benefit analysis before hiring an appraiser. If you do decide to go ahead with an appraisal, make sure you specify the official appraisal date (June 30, 1990—not the current date!) for which you want the appraisal.

On the Market in the Base Period

If your property was on the market in the base period, *but did not sell*, it probably was not worth the asking price. You should be able to substantiate the upper limit of its value to the assessor with a copy of a listing agreement, dated MLS brochure, or even a dated newspaper advertisement—anything which proves it was on the market and states the asking price. If you received a written offer on the property, submit that information as well, or a sworn statement by you to that effect.

Additions or Improvements

Assessors add the value of additions or improvements made to your property, by you or a prior owner, to your appraisal via the information on a building permit. It is your responsibility to make an accurate and valid determination of the *market value*—as opposed to cost—of those additions or improvements. You might want to contact an appraiser for written estimates of the market value of the addition or improvement.

For example, a swimming pool which cost $15,000 to build will probably not actually increase the property's value by $15,000. Also, if a building permit was pulled by you or a former owner, but the work was never completed, there is a good chance that the value shown on the permit has been added to your appraisal anyway, as some assessors may not have had the time or money to confirm construction.

Equalization

Every method described thus far has concentrated on sale prices. Equalization, however, involves comparing the assessor's appraised value of your property with the *assessor's appraised values*—not sale prices—of properties similar to your own. It is the one method expressly designed to ensure that property owners are not charged any more in property taxes than their neighbors owning similar properties.

Go to the assessor's office and obtain the appraised values ("Total Actual Value") of all properties similar to your own in your neighborhood. Date of sale is not considered in equalization. Appraised values are a matter of public record, so just give the assessor a list of the addresses for the properties you identified in your research.

Unbuildable Lots

You may be able to substantially reduce the assessor's appraised value of certain lots if they meet *any one* of the following criteria:

— The lot is too small to build a house on, as defined by zoning standards.
— The lot does not qualify for a well permit (assumes no public supply is available).
— The lot is too small to qualify for a septic system permit (assumes a public sewer system is unavailable).
— The lot is land-locked: The property is totally surrounded by other properties, thereby preventing normal access.

Should you have an unbuildable lot, obtain statements from the proper zoning and/or water authorities certifying the above criteria.

Income/Expenses

If you are a commercial/industrial property owner using the Income Approach, you should collect the following information:

Tax Returns

It may be helpful to have your 1989 or 1990 tax returns available for review to prove your income and expenses. Only you or, with your permission, your agent, can access the return if the return is left with the assessor.

Lease Rates

You may also want to have copies of your leases available. Extensive information on lease rates per square foot (see Appendix W) may be available through assessors, commercial Realtors, or, for Front Range commercial properties, through Dresco, Inc., (303) 691-9085, and the Building Owners and Management Association (B.O.M.A.) at (303) 820-2662.

Capitalization Rates

Collect capitalization rates of other "sold" properties for properties similar to yours from the listing brokers, as this is where most of the discussion with assessors will concentrate. Also contact your assessor to find out what cap rate he/she is using for your type of property, as well as a commercial appraiser, or the Building Owners and Management Association (B.O.M.A.) at (303) 820-2662 for possible help.

Vacancy Rate

You may need to obtain average vacancy rates (see Appendix X). The more localized the information is, the better. This information is available through several sources:

— The assessor's office—Be sure to ask *how* they obtained their data.
— Commercial property management companies (refer to local Yellow Page listings)
— Commercial Realtors
— Building Owners and Managers Association (B.O.M.A.) —(303) 820-266
— Dresco, Inc.—(303) 691-9085

Chapter 8

ANALYZE THE DATA THROUGH ONE OR MORE METHODS

After you have collected all your information, analyze it. Be reasonable and fair. You can either use the *lowest* values you have obtained in your research (some assessors will use the highest ones), or average the sale prices together. If, in your analysis, you find you are in disagreement with the assessor's appraisal of your property, you should file a protest.

Comparables Method

Compare the assessor's appraisal of your property with the sale prices of the comparables you have collected. Look primarily at comparables from the base period, and only at those which are most similar to your property (style, general size, general age, etc.).

Another point to remember is that you *can* adjust sale prices through the entire base period to their values as of June 30, 1990, the last day of the base period and official appraisal date.

Property owners using the cost approach should add together the land value and depreciated building value to determine the current replacement cost. They can then continue, following the steps outlined below.

Compare properties

Drive by the comparable properties for which you have obtained addresses to ensure that they do represent fair comparisons to your property. Take pictures of the properties. If a comparable property was sold by a Realtor, you could even go a step further and contact him/her (names available through MLS "sold" data from a Realtor) for additional information about that property which may help you.

Consider how the properties compare to yours. Are they in better condition? In a nicer subdivision than yours? Do the other properties have any special features, such as a swimming pool or sprinkler system? Look at floor plans, too. For example, a second bath will generally increase a property's value more if installed off the master bedroom than if added in the basement. Or, a home with two bedrooms on one level and a third on another is generally worth less than a home with all three bedrooms on one level—even if both homes carry the same overall square footage.

Commercial property owners: Do the comparables have more acreage? A railroad spur? Better location?

Also make notes on any physical weaknesses in your own property, such as a cracked basement. Is your property next to a railroad track? On a busy street? Note these and any other comments about the properties.

Obtain a comprehensive list

If, after your checking, you find that the list of comparable properties you receive from the assessor is not really comparable, go back and request another, more comprehensive, list. Keep the erroneous list, though, because the assessor might unknowingly be using these very properties to defend his/her position!

The more good comparables you obtain, the better position you will be in to substantiate the value of your property. The only comparable information the assessor can use to defend his/her appraisal of your property is the sale price of properties similar to yours. You are entitled to the same information as the assessor.

Give the best comparables the most weight in deciding what your property should be worth. If the sale prices of the best comparables and your own appraisal are about the same, and you have already verified and corrected your appraisal card data, chances are good that your appraisal is a fair one. Before deciding not to protest your appraisal, though, reread the section on Equalization.

Foreclosures

If you have turned up some foreclosures (sold by a lending entity) in your research, use care in weighing them. If you have found only one foreclosure among four or five good comparables, don't put much weight in it. On the other hand, if two or three of your best comparables turn out to be foreclosures, they deserve considerable weight in your analysis.

Price-per-Square-Foot

If the calculated price per square foot on your property is higher than the price per square foot on the properties from the list of comparable properties you have obtained, you will probably want to file a protest.

Purchase Price

If you are using the purchase price method, your analysis is simple. As explained, the assessor's appraisal of your property should be no more than what you paid for it. If it is higher, consider protesting. Be sure and use this method if you can. It is usually the best indicator of value.

Price-per-Unit

If the assessor's calculated price per unit on your property is higher than the price per unit rate on other properties from the list of comparable apartment buildings you have obtained, you will probably want to file a protest.

Other Appraisals

If other appraisals of your property are lower than the assessor's appraisal of your property, you will want to file a protest. These other appraisals can often be used successfully to bring the assessor's appraisal down to their level.

On the Market in the Base Period

If the assessor's appraisal of your property is higher than the price for which you *attempted* to sell your property, the assessor should reduce your appraisal to at least the level at which you attempted to sell. If you received a written offer, use it to reduce your appraisal even further.

Additions or Improvements

Most additions and improvements do not increase the value of the property by the amount they actually cost to build. If you (or a prior owner) have made an addition or improvement to your property, it is important to look at its *market* value, not cost.

For instance, in the case of the swimming pool which *cost* $15,000 to build, the value it added to the property might be only $3,000 or less. If the assessor used the cost approach in valuing the pool, as could be expected, the appraisal would be artificially high. Consider protesting your appraisal if this or any other similar situation applies to you.

Equalization

Remember that equalization deals with assessors' appraisals, not sale prices, and can be used for all types of properties. If the assessor's *appraisal* of similar properties is lower than the *appraisal* on your property, you should consider protesting, using equalization (not sale prices) as your basis for protest.

For instance, your neighbors may have the same kind of house as yours. You will probably find, however, that the assessor's appraisal of your neighbors' house is lower than yours. You can protest to bring the assessor's appraisal of your property down to the level of your neighbors'—regardless of either property's true value.

So, let's assume your property and your neighbors' similar properties carry fair market values of $90,000. The assessor appraises some of your neighbors' properties at $80,000, but yours at $90,000. In that case, you have the right to have your appraisal dropped to $80,000. I think you will find this frequently happens.

Unbuildable Lots
The appraisal on an unbuildable lot should be close to zero ($0). If you have a lot which is unbuildable according to the definitions described earlier in this book, you should consider filing a protest.

Income/Expenses
Property owners using the Income Approach may use one or both of the following techniques to analyze their tax positions:

Capitalization rates
Determine the average cap rate for properties similar to yours from the data you have collected. Use the highest cap rate that is appropriate and defensible—the average or your own actual rate—to determine your property's value. If your value then turns out to be lower than the assessor's appraisal (perhaps due to the cap rate the assessor is using), you should consider protesting.

Vacancy rates
Determine the average vacancy rate for buildings similar to yours from the data collected. Use the highest vacancy rate that is appropriate and defensible—the average or your own actual rate—to determine your property's value. If the value arrived at is lower than the assessor's appraisal (perhaps due to the vacancy rate the assessor is using), you should consider protesting.

Chapter 9

FILE A FIRST-ROUND PROTEST (ASSESSOR)

Protesting an inaccurate appraisal can make a real difference in your tax bill. If you reduce the assessor's appraisal by 10 percent, your upcoming tax bill will be 10 percent less than what it would have been otherwise.

Also, the volume of protests itself can often make a difference. If assessors receive a large number of protests from a particular subdivision, for example, they may realize that those homes' appraisals are indeed inaccurate. The assessors would be more likely, then, to correct the situation *en masse* the following year.

Basis of Protest

Property owners can protest in five ways:

1. The assessor's total appraisal (land and building)
2. The land-only appraisal value
3. The improvement-only appraisal value (buildings)
4. Equalization
5. Appraisal errors

Unless you have a good reason, do not use (2) above. Some assessors get *very* defensive on land-only protests.

There is no fee to file a protest.

When to Protest

You may file a protest with your county assessor in May. *Written protests* must be postmarked no later than May 27. *In-person protests* may be filed during business hours any time in May. An in-person protest will insure more attention to your case.

If you find yourself short on time to prepare your protest, you can simply let your assessor know, in writing or in person, that you wish to protest. All you need to do is write a short note stating that you are protesting your valuation. You need not use any special form. You will probably get a denial notice if you take this action, but it will preserve your right to protest in the *second* round.

If you do not make the deadlines for protest, there is now another way to protest. In effect, you can protest year-round with your first protest attempt in the two-year reappraisal period. You must use the "Petition for Abatement or Refund of Taxes" form (see Appendix J) and state your reason for protest as "valuation," not appraisal card errors, etc. Some assessors will hold this type of protest and address it in 1992; others will process it immediately. Either way, you will be notified.

A word of caution: The legislature may eliminate this "back-door" approach at any time. Call the State Division of Property Taxation at (303) 866-2371 for an update before trying it.

How to File

You should have received a protest form with your reappraisal notice of value. You do not need to use the form to file a protest. Any note expressing the thought will do.

Some assessors' protest forms are multi-purpose forms. Only the "Real Property" section applies to real estate. Commercial/industrial and apartment building property owners may also want to review and learn about the "Personal Property" section of the form with the assessor, and can purchase a copy of the Assessors' Reference Manual on Personal Property Valuation for $25 from the State Division of Property Taxation at (303) 866-2371.

Whether you use the assessor's form or not, you need to document your position. The assessor will often determine appraisals on the cost basis during the course of the protest process. Because the market approach will almost always be more accurate *and* lower than the cost approach, it is more appropriate, in the interest of fairness, to use the market approach.

It is almost impossible to prove or defend the cost approach. Ask the assessor what approach he/she is using, and how he/she determined the value. Usually, the more emphasis an assessor places on the cost approach, the weaker his/her position.

If you noted a "neighborhood adjustment" (NHAJ) on the calculations you requested from the assessor when obtaining your list of sales, bring this to the attention of the assessor in your protest, whether your protest is in writing or in person. Since this adjustment most likely indicates a figure calculated to make the market approach and cost approach results match, do not hesitate to remind him/her of the fairness of the market approach—without the unfairness of using the NHAJ.

Include as much supporting documentation as possible in your protest. Make sure the property identification number is on every piece of paper you prepare. Include information on all good comparables, not just the best ones. Include *all* the comparables you have-one or a dozen. An assessor typically has three or four comparables for his/her defense.

Vacant Lots
"Request to Combine Properties"
Form (Appendix Y)

At any time, you may file this form to obtain a reduction in land valuations if you own a vacant lot. Specifically, you may be able to consolidate a vacant lot with your adjacent home (or other residential dwelling) lot for tax valuation purposes. Or, if you own several pieces of vacant land, you can combine them into one tax bill. Either way, they must be contiguous, be in the same taxing districts, and have the same exact ownership.

The principle of lot, or land, consolidation is based on diminishing purchase price (value) per lot. That is, the value of each site will generally decrease as the number of sites purchased together increases. For example, if one lot costs $25,000, three lots purchased together would not necessarily cost $75,000. Note that consolidation of vacant lots does not affect the salability or current fair market value of the lots. At the time you sell one of the contiguous lots, the assessor then recreates two separate files, generating two separate tax bills.

In addition, remember that the assessment rate on vacant residential land is 29 percent. If you can combine a vacant residential lot with the lot on which a house is built, your assessment rate on the combined lots will be 14.34 percent (the current residential assessment rate). That would reduce your taxes by almost half—or even more, because a few assessors put one value on a lot, regardless of its size.

Chapter 10

EVALUATING THE ASSESSOR'S ANSWER

First-Round Protest Results

You can expect to receive a letter notifying you of the results of your protest in late June or early July. If you do not receive a notice on or before the last working day in June, though, call the assessor. Make sure your protest, as well as the result, was recorded.

If you are in agreement with the assessor's decision, your work is done. As a few assessors do not record corrections permanently, be aware that you may need to repeat the process in 1993.

If you have waited to protest until 1992, however, and win, the correction will not automatically be retroactive to the previous year (1991). To obtain a refund on the 1991 taxes, you are required to file a "Petition for Abatement or Refund of Taxes" form (see Appendix J). You can usually obtain this form through your assessor's office.

Deciding to Appeal the First-Round Decision

If you are in disagreement with the assessor's decision, you have the right to file a second-round protest (50,000 protests were filed in 1989). Regardless of the decision, the assessor's written answer does not mean he/she has actually reviewed your case. Should you be denied in the first round, take your case to the second—and third, if necessary—rounds of protest. It is only then that many assessors begin to take protests seriously.

If you decide to take your protest to the second round, you have only a few days in which to notify the Board of Equalization (County Commissioners). Look for the deadline in your first-round denial notice. If you do not notify the Board as instructed, you will lose your right to protest any further, and then must accept whatever your tax bill is next January.

If you are denied in the first round, and believe you have a good case, I encourage you to file a second-round protest. You have an excellent chance of winning your protest if you continue to the second, then third rounds.

Negotiation

At any time in the protest process, you may find that the assessor offers to reduce your appraisal. This happens most commonly at the beginning of the hearing in the second or third rounds, and usually because the assessor does not have enough data to defend his/her position.

In such a situation, the assessor (or, on occasion, the county commissioners) will offer you a "stipulation," or a flat offer to accept a lower valuation. If you accept this offer, your appraisal will be reduced accordingly and you then forfeit any additional right to protest until next year. A stipulation is only good for the year in which it is accepted.

If you accept a stipulation during your protest in 1992, remember to file a "Petition for Abatement or Refund of Taxes" form (see Appendix J) in 1992 to obtain a refund on 1991 taxes. Any corrections made to your valuation are not automatically retroactive to the previous year.

If you choose to reject the offer, the hearing will continue as scheduled. In almost all cases, the hearing officer will not rule higher than the assessor's offer. Depending on your case, you may have a chance to reduce your appraisal further than the offer.

As stated before, the burden of proof is on the property owner. In the second round of protest, however, the assessor will also be trying to prove his/her position. If it appears that both you and the assessor have good cases, be willing to negotiate for a middle ground if an offer is made to you—but not until then.

Assessor Practices

During the protest process, keep in mind that, as a property owner, you have the *right* to protest the appraisal. A few assessors may lead you to believe otherwise, because too many assessment errors discovered by property owners will require them to reappraise their entire counties at enormous costs and embarrassment.

For example, the assessor may point out that your property's appraisal falls in line with the overall neighborhood average, and therefore is correct. This is simply a reference to the Mass Appraisal Method of calculations used to determine appraisals and has no bearing on an individual's property evaluation. This is exactly the reason for which the state legislature and assessment system set up the protest procedure: to allow property owners to correct errors on *individual appraisals.*

Assessors might also say that they cannot change your appraisal because it meets "auditors' guidelines," because "the auditor won't let us," or because your appraisal "fits the sales ratio analysis" or "coefficient of dispersion" parameters. *None* of these defenses have anything to do with the valuation of your property. Continue with your protest.

Some assessors may argue that they cannot change appraisals for fear of defeating the principle of equalization, which states that identical properties should be appraised equally. If your assessor uses this defense, he/she may just be trying to avoid correcting the appraisal. The assessor is assuming that properties are identical and if he/she corrects the valuation of one property, then he/she will have to change the valuations of *all* similar properties in the area.

The fallacy of that position is that no two properties are the same. It is unlikely that two properties would be so identical to justify a mass change in valuation for an error you detected. But if your error *is* reflected in other similar properties, the assessor *should* reduce the valuations of all those properties in the interest of fairness and equalization.

Take a condominium complex as an example. At first glance, it might appear that every unit is the same. But take a closer look. The third-story unit in a building without an elevator is usually worth less than a first-story unit. The unit that backs up to the highway has less value than the unit which overlooks a courtyard. The point is that you should not accept an assessor's defense of equalization if you believe your appraisal is incorrect. Do not pay more than your fair share.

Some assessors might argue that you should not use foreclosures to defend your position because their values represent run-down properties. In fact, the foreclosing entities (banks, HUD, etc.) usually fix up the properties before offering them to the public for sale.

Assessors may also claim that if they lower your valuation, everyone else's taxes will increase. That is not the issue. If an assessor makes this comment, he/she is, in effect, making a public statement that you are supposed to pay more than your fair share. Remember that you are not the only property owner conducting a protest. It is only through use of the protest system by concerned individuals that property owners can hope to achieve fairness throughout the entire system—and avoid paying hundreds or thousands of dollars more than their fair share.

Be aware that a few assessors will defend their positions or deny your protest, even if you are absolutely right. If you encounter this situation, remember that you have several more rounds of protest available to you. Also see "Complaints," Chapter 15.

Chapter 11

FILE A SECOND-ROUND PROTEST (Board of Equalization)

Instructions for applying to the second round of protest will be outlined in your first-round denial notice. Generally, you simply mail in the form within a specified time period, and wait to hear when your second round is scheduled.

The second round is a meeting with the Board of Equalization: county commissioners or their representatives, called hearing officers (see Appendix Z). This round may create a fairer and more complete review of your protest than the first round. If hearing officers are utilized by your county commissioners, they will make recommendations to the commissioners on each case after hearing both the assessor's and property owner's positions.

If hearing officers are used, you want them to possess a strong background in property appraisals. Before going into the hearing, you can ask an official in charge about the hearing officer's qualifications and specific real estate appraisal background and experience (i.e., Has he/she done this exclusively for a living?). In Jefferson County, for example, these officers are usually attorneys, former county employees, or former assessors, rather than appraisers who would be more informed. If the officer does not have the desired background, you should request another hearing with a more knowledgeable officer.

The Hearing

The hearing is simply a meeting and nothing of which to be afraid. Do not be surprised to see the same assessor personnel at this and other rounds of protest. In this hearing, the property owner begins by stating his/her position to the county commissioners; be sure to tell the commissioners what you think your value should be and why. *Do not talk about taxes.* The assessor then states his/her position. Note that you will receive a copy of the assessor's worksheet containing the comparable data he/she is using to defend his/her valuation.

The assessor might also state the weaknesses of your position, and you should be prepared to state the weaknesses of his/her position, as well as defend your own position. The commissioners can ask questions of both you and the assessor. Be aware that a few assessors may stretch to find weaknesses in your position, like claiming that your sales must have been foreclosure sales—when, in fact, he/she has no idea.

After you and the assessor have stated your cases to the commissioners, each of you will have the opportunity to ask questions of the other. You and the assessor will then make final statements to the commissioners. In your final statement, recap your strong points as well as any good reasons you have to believe that the assessor's data is wrong. You will be notified of the commissioners' decision by mail within 30 days.

Preparation

Once you elect to go to the second round, you can take additional action to prepare. When you send in the form to protest in the second round, ask for the assessor's documentation that will be used against you at the hearing. Assessors are now required by law to provide this information to you, *upon request,* 48 hours prior to the hearing. You, however, do not need to submit anything before this hearing.

Drive by and research the properties to ensure that they are good comparisons to your property, and to identify the assessor's weak comparables or other mistakes.

You can add, change, or delete material used in the first round of protest in this round. For example, you can research each of the assessor's comparables before the hearing by looking at their appraised valuations, not the sale prices (see "Equalization" in Chapter 8. To go "the extra mile," obtain photo copies of the comparable properties' "sold" data from a Realtor in your area. Contact the Realtor who listed the property (from the MLS data) and ask for any additional information which might help your case: views, property condition at time of sale, etc.

Also, obtain the appraisal cards for each of the assessor's comparables. Check the accuracy of the appraisal card data with MLS brochure information. Finally, attend other hearings. They are open to the public and it will build your confidence as well as help improve your case.

Bring four extra copies of all your documentation to the hearing; give one to the assessor and keep one for yourself. Make sure the original goes to a county commissioner. If there is more than one commissioner, provide each with a copy.

Once at the hearing, do not allow (object!) the assessor to introduce any additional evidence other than that provided to you 48 hours before the hearing.

Chapter 12

FILE A THIRD-ROUND PROTEST

Should you be denied in the second round, I encourage you to continue your protest. In the third round, you have three choices of appeal: the Board of Assessment Appeals (B.A.A.); District Court; or arbitration.

Board of Assessment Appeals

Should you be denied in the second round, you are encouraged to file for the third round of protest with the B.A.A. In 1989, property owners filed an estimated 11,000 B.A.A. third-round protests. In this hearing, the county has no influence. Over 60 percent of cases heard received reductions. By law, your valuation cannot be increased at this hearing.

Instructions will be contained in the second-round denial notice. Generally, the property owner will be instructed to call the B.A.A. at (303) 866-5880 to request a packet of information. When received, complete the two-page document within 30 days of receiving your decision from the Board of Equalization (second-round decision).

The third-round B.A.A. hearing is very similar to the second round in style. Typically, a panel of two hearing officers will hear your protest. A county attorney will represent the commissioners and use the assessor as a witness. There are no fees involved in this round.

To prepare for the hearing, which will be conducted in downtown Denver, review all the comparables the assessor gave you at previous hearings for errors or discrepancies. Ten days before the hearing, you and the assessor must submit to the B.A.A., and to each other, all data which will be used at the hearing. No additional written evidence can be used at the hearing. You and the assessor can, however, submit additional verbal evidence. You can now use equalization as an additional defense.

You can represent yourself in this round, or employ the services of an attorney or tax agent (see Appendix F). Actually, anyone with your written permission may represent you. Using an attorney may or may not be cost-effective. Identify the amount of your tax savings for which you are striving and compare it with the cost of the attorney.

You may also bring in an expert witness(es) in support of your case. If you do use expert witnesses, be aware that they can only answer questions posed directly to them at this hearing. Prepare your questions carefully, and in such a way as to obtain the information you want the hearing officers to know.

Your hearing will be scheduled within a few months of filing. You will be notified by mail at least 30 days in advance of the hearing. Thirteen days before your hearing, pick up from the assessor the assessor's position and review it prior to your 10-day deadline to submit your data.

Hearings are open to the public. Attending one or two will make you more comfortable with the process.

If you conduct your protest in 1992, and are successful in this round, do not forget to file a "Petition for Abatement or Refund of Taxes" form (see Appendix J) to obtain the refund on your 1991 taxes.

District Court

District Court is expensive, risky, and generally utilized only with large commercial properties, large apartment buildings, or large land holdings. Your third-round denial notice will provide more information.

Call a property tax attorney (see Appendix F) for additional advice on this procedure.

Arbitration

After you meet with the Board of Equalization (second round), you could choose to go to arbitration instead of the B.A.A. or District Court. If you choose this route, it will be your last form of protest. You can not advance further if you do not agree with the decision.

Arbitration carries a maximum cost of $150 (for residential properties), usually payable in the form of a deposit by the property owner. Fees for all other types of properties are as agreed to by the parties involved. After the hearing takes place, the arbitrator will make a final determination on the payment allocation between the parties involved; the property owner may end up receiving a full or partial refund.

If you do choose arbitration, check the qualifications of the potential arbitrators carefully. The list of potential arbitrators is a county commissioner-approved list. It is possible that the arbitrator you choose may be the hearing officer you just had. Try to obtain a real estate appraiser who has experience and qualifications with the type of property you own (e.g., residential, commercial, agricultural). The format of the hearing is the same as that of the second round of protest.

If you win your protest through arbitration in 1992, do not forget to file the "Petition for Abatement or Refund of Taxes" form (see Appendix J) to obtain your refund on last year's taxes.

The use of arbitration is on the decline in Colorado, primarily because of its risk, cost, and the improved speed in scheduling third-round B.A.A. hearings. This year, B.A.A. hearings are being scheduled and held four times faster than previous years. In addition, use of the third-round B.A.A. protest leaves the door open for the fourth round if necessary; once you go to arbitration, you forfeit your right to all future rounds of protest for this year.

I recommend arbitration only if the arbitrator (hearing officer) is a real estate appraiser for the type of property you own, and if you are already experienced in and comfortable with the protest and assessment system. I do not recommend it in general, and definitely not for property owners filing a protest for the first time.

Chapter 13

FILE A FOURTH-ROUND PROTEST
(Court of Appeals)

You may go to the Court of Appeals only after a third-round decision of the B.A.A. or District Court has been made. The Court provides a judicial review of your case, reading the transcripts of the third-round B.A.A. or District Court hearing and reviewing the documentation to determine if facts are true and the law was followed. No new information can be presented here.

Call a property tax attorney for additional advice on this procedure (see Appendix F).

Chapter 14

TAX CREDITS AND DEFERRALS FOR SENIORS

Tax Credits for Seniors

The State of Colorado offers a property tax *refund* program for qualifying seniors. Form 104-PTC and additional information may be obtained from your county treasurer (see Appendix Z). Qualifications are:

1. Form 104-PTC must be filed with the Colorado income tax return.
2. The applicant must be at least 65 years old (58 for a surviving spouse), or disabled as to a degree for full benefits from a bona fide source.
3. The applicant must have been a full-year resident of Colorado.
4. The applicant must have paid one of the following:
   — a general property tax
   — rent on a property on which general property tax was paid
   — rent to a public housing authority
   — rent on a mobile home or space to house a mobile home
5. A single applicant can not have income over $7,500. A married couple can not have income over $11,200.

Note: In addition to the state program, many cities in Colorado have their own tax credit programs for seniors (see Appendix AA). If you live within boundaries of a city, check with your city government office for information.

Tax Deferrals for Seniors

The State of Colorado offers a property tax deferral program for seniors who meet the following qualifications. Note that this is a *deferral* program. Taxes must be paid at some point in the future (see below). Obtain the application for deferral of property taxes from your county treasurer (see Appendix Z).

1. The taxpayer must be 65 years old or older by January 1 of the year in which the application is made.
2. The taxpayer must own (or be purchasing) and live in the property on which the taxes will be deferred.
3. Property taxes must not be income-producing, and there can be no delinquent taxes.
4. The application must be filed between January 1 and April 1 of each year in which the deferral is to be used. You must re-apply each year for additional deferments.
5. The taxpayer must obtain the assessed value of the property from his/her county assessor (see Appendix I). Once the deferred taxes plus accrued interest is more than market value of property, no other deferrals can be made.
6. The property must not be subject to a lien or deed which has been recorded for less than five years, unless the property owner has applied for a deferral in prior years, or if the property owner makes an agreement of record to subordinate the lien or deed to the State for deferred taxes.

When an application for deferral is accepted, the county treasurer will record the application and send it to the state treasurer. The state treasurer will then pay the county treasurer and hold a lien on the property with eight percent interest per year.

The total amount of deferred property tax and accrued interest is due and payable one year after the death of the taxpayer (unless the spouse continues deferral), or 90 days after the sale or transfer of the property. When full payment is received, the state treasurer will send a release of lien to whomever makes the payment.

For additional information on either credits or deferrals, contact your county treasurer (see Appendix Z), or the Colorado Department of Revenue at (303) 534-1209.

Chapter 15

COMPLAINTS

If, at any time, you have complaints or problems which can not be resolved, you have several effective alternative courses of action:

— Contact the State Property Tax Administrator at (303) 866-2371. It is his/her responsibility to follow up on complaints from the public. His/Her staff is the best overall source of information on property tax assessment questions, and appears to have no bias in favor of the assessors.

— Write a letter to the editor(s) of your local newspaper(s) (see Appendix BB) to alert other members of the community to the problem. State your position clearly, remembering that the people with the power to effect change in the system—including your local legislators—read your local papers.

— Contact your county assessor (see Appendix I). He/She may not even be aware of the problem.

— Contact your county commissioners (see Appendix Z). They exert direct control on the opinions and operations of the Board of Equalization (and, indirectly, the assessor).

— Contact your state legislators (see Appendices CC and DD).

— Exercise your right to vote: All county assessors (except Denver's) are up for reelection in November, 1994. If last year's elections were any indication, the system does work!

Chapter 16

COLORADO'S PROPERTY TAX ASSESSMENT SYSTEM: Problems and Solutions

This chapter is devoted to examining some of the most glaring problems I have found in Colorado's property tax assessment system. Along with a description and explanation of the problems I see, I am offering some suggestions for solving the problems. It is my hope that the appropriate state agencies and departments, assessors, county commissioners, and legislators will use this chapter to better our system by reducing protests and the associated costs. If you're in agreement, please call your state senator (see Appendix CC), and state representative (see Appendix DD), and write a letter to the editor of your local newspaper (see Appendix BB).

1. The Problem
Appraisal card information is inaccurate.

Why the Problem Needs to be Addressed

- With over two million properties and property appraisal cards to update (see Appendix A), mistakes are bound to be made. The extent of the mistakes is clear: In 1989, $27 million of tax money was refunded to 16,167 property owners due to errors (see Appendix B). The average refund was $1,675.

- According to my survey of Colorado's 11 largest counties, 1 out of every 3 properties in the state was over-appraised and overtaxed in 1987. Seventeen percent of all properties in the state—340,000 properties—were overtaxed 5-100 percent. The 175,000 protests conducted in 1989 alone (see Appendix A) suggest that many of these properties were valued too high due to appraisal card errors.

- In the late 1970s, a county assessor admitted to me that 70 percent of the appraisal cards in his county were incorrect.

- Almost all appraisals are "office appraisals," based on appraisal card data and not on physical inspections. Assessors rarely see the interior of a property or measure the exterior of a house. They can not even afford to conduct very many drive-by appraisals.

- While it is the owner's responsibility to notify the assessor of inaccuracies on the appraisal card, most property owners are not even aware of the appraisal card's existence—let alone what data it includes or how important it is.

The Proposed Solution

Mail appraisal card information to all property owners every two years to reinforce the owner's responsibility to detect errors.

Boulder County already has sent out appraisal card information with each reappraisal. Bill Goodyear, the former Boulder County assessor, was sincerely surprised at how honest the public was in responding to the information.

The Benefits

- The accuracy of the property tax assessment system will be improved most dramatically by improving the accuracy of the appraisal card.

- Since over $2 billion is collected from Colorado taxpayers each year in property taxes (see Appendix D), improved accuracy is a worthwhile benefit to taxpayers and the assessment community alike.

- More accurate appraisal card information means the assessor's appraisal is much more likely to be accurate, thereby resulting in fewer protests.
- More accurate appraisal card information means fewer people will be overtaxed.
- When a property is sold, the sale price of that property is used to help determine the appraisal values of all similar properties in the neighborhood or county. More accurate appraisal card information would improve overall neighborhood and county appraisals substantially.
- Colorado's appraisal card information will need to be updated at some time, no matter what. It would be much more cost-effective and realistic to mail the information to property owners and ask them to review their own, rather than to send out assessor personnel to each property. That process would take at least several decades to complete at a cost exceeding $20 million dollars.

2. The Problem
Current audit guidelines and techniques, when applied on a county-wide basis, contribute to inaccurate appraisals.

Why the Problem Needs to be Addressed
- Each county in the state is audited by Thimgan and Associates, (303) 985-8820, to check for overall accuracy in appraisals, using a sales ratio analysis and a coefficient of dispersion test. As it stands now, individual subdivisions or areas may have gross errors in appraisal, but if the entire county average falls within minimum audit guidelines, less attention will be given to those areas.
- If the sales ratio analysis and coefficient techniques were applied to subdivisions rather than entire counties, then those subdivisions which failed the audit would receive attention from the assessor for corrections.

- Most counties are simply too large to expect a county-wide rating to be purposeful.
- Most counties are too diverse in age, price range, or other factors to expect a county-wide rating to be purposeful.

The Proposed Solution

Modify state audit guidelines to include a provision for subdivisions (categorized and audited according to age, square feet, etc.) to be audited with a sales ratio test, *as well as* the coefficient of dispersion test on both sold and unsold properties.

The Benefits

- Assessors' appraisals would be more accurate throughout each county.
- Property owners living in distinct areas would have a better opportunity to receive fair consideration in appraisal valuation.
- The number of protests and associated costs would be reduced.

3. **The Problem**

Over one-third of the properties throughout the state are appraised higher than the actual sale price of the property, according to eleven 1987 and one 1990 sales ratio reports.

Why the Problem Needs to be Addressed

- Sales ratio analysis reports (available at any county assessor's office), designed to assist legislators in checking overall accuracy of the property tax assessment system, compare the sale prices of properties which sold in the base period to the assessor's appraised values. In general, appraisal values should not be higher than the sale prices.

The Proposed Solution

- Require a review of any properties with an assessor's appraisal (actual value) greater than or equal to five percent above the sale price, per the sales ratio analysis report.

- Require physical inspections of any properties with an appraisal value greater than or equal to 10 percent above the sale price.

The Benefits
- The number of complaints and protests from property owners will be reduced significantly.
- The overall accuracy of the appraisal of the properties in question, as well as of all similar properties in the state (half a million), will be improved.

4. The Problem
The coefficient of dispersion is too high.

Why the Problem Needs to be Addressed
- The purpose of the coefficient of dispersion is to keep a county within limits of accuracy in appraisal valuation. Current law allows an error of 15.99 percent above the norm on residential properties, meaning that a county can be overvalued by 15.99 percent. On commercial and vacant land classifications, the coefficient is 20.99 percent.
- In 1988, I visited nearly a dozen assessor's offices around the state and asked the staff for recommendations on improving the system. Almost without exception, appraisers suggested lowering the coefficient to improve the system.
- There are some poorly appraised classifications and subclassifications in each county.

The Proposed Solution
Lower the audit coefficient of dispersion to 5 percent on residential properties, and to 10 percent on all commercial and vacant land classifications for both sold and unsold properties.

The Benefits
- Lowering the rates would dramatically increase the accuracy of appraisals.
- Lowering the rates would allow assessors the opportunity, without further legislation, to improve their appraisal

methods in those classifications in which they are weak.

- The number of protests—and associated costs—would be reduced.
- Lowering the rates would improve fairness. The current situation allows for theoretical discrepancies of as much as 38 percent on residential classification tax bills and up to 53 percent on commercial and vacant land classifications.

5. The Problem

Actual values of the sold comparables used as a defense against the property owner are typically not disclosed by assessors at second-round (Board of Equalization) or third-round (Board of Assessment Appeals) hearings.

Why the Problem Needs to be Addressed

- Disclosure of the assessor's appraised values (equalization) on comparable properties can be critical to the property owner's case. Although the comparables' appraised values may often fall substantially below the sale price, assessors may be disclosing only the sale price as a defense against the taxpayer.

The Proposed Solution

Require assessors to disclose appraisal values whenever they report sales data (at hearings, or any other time they communicate such data to the public).

The Benefits

- Second and third rounds of protest would become fairer if both the assessor and property owner have knowledge and use of the same information.

6. The Problem

The definition of "equalization" is inconsistent.

Why the Problem Needs to be Addressed

- Most hearing officers, county commissioners, assessors, and others seem to have different opinions on the definition of the term.

- The lack of clarity and consistency is unfair to the property owner. He/she is often at the mercy of the opinion of the hearing officers', assessors', or county commissioners' interpretations.

The Proposed Solution
Develop a clear and consistent definition of "equalization."

The Benefits
- A clear definition would increase the effectiveness of this method within the system.
- A clear definition would serve to increase fairness to the property owner.

7. The Problem
Property owners are not advised of their right to apply for multi-year tax refunds when they win their protests on the basis of appraisal card errors (or if they conduct their initial appraisal or equalization protest in 1992).

Why the Problem Needs to be Addressed
- The current system is unjust: If the assessor discovers omitted property (i.e., unknown house), he/she can collect up to six years' worth of taxes for the error. If a property owner discovers an error in his/her appraisal, he/she is eligible for an abatement or refund of only up to two years—and oftentimes, does not even know he/she can do this!
- It is time-consuming enough for property owners to review and correct their property appraisal cards. At the very least, assessors should inform them of their right to try and recover back taxes paid on errors detected.

The Proposed Solution
Require the assessor to notify property owners of their right to apply for a multi-year refund when they conduct successful protests.

The Benefits
- More property owners would be able to receive the refunds due them. Just in 1989, property owners who

were aware of their rights claimed over $27 million in
refunds (see Appendices B, C, and G).
- By keeping taxpayers informed of their rights, the
  system would become more fair.

8. The Problem
The refund/abatement period is only two years (before
January 1, 1990, it was six years), and is applied inconsis-
tently.

Why the Problem Needs to be Addressed
- It is time-consuming enough for property owners to
  review and correct their property appraisals. A two-year
  abatement on an error on which the taxpayer has been
  paying for years is too little compensation.
- The current system is unjust: If a property owner
  discovers an error in his/her appraisal, he/she is eligible
  for an abatement or refund of up to two years. However, if the assessor discovers omitted property (i.e., an
  unknown cabin), he/she can collect up to six years'
  worth of taxes for the error.
- When a property owner wins a protest, the assessor
  corrects the appraisal, but often does not tell the taxpayer that he/she might be entitled to a refund/abatement.
  Some property owners learn of the refund/abatement
  provision three or four years down the line—too late to
  apply for it. Most never learn about it.
- Although the State Division of Property Taxation's
  interpretation of the refund/abatement period is two
  years, many county commissioners use only a one-year
  window. Most taxpayers do not know there is a difference of opinion between the state and some counties.

The Proposed Solution
- Modify current law clearly to allow everyone an imme-
  diate two-year refund.
- Restore the six-year refund period.

The Benefits
- More property owners would be able to receive the millions of dollars in refunds due them.
- The system would be equally just to both the assessor and the property owner.

9. The Problem
Assessors include the highest property sale prices in their calculations to determine the appraised value of *all* properties in a given area or for a given type of property, resulting in an increased volume of protests.

Why the Problem Needs to be Addressed
- Typical homes should not be appraised by the same standards as the finest homes in the neighborhood; i.e., they should not be subject to the same sale price calculations as the top homes.
- Properties which command the top sale prices in an area above the prevailing prices usually do so for good reason: they are in outstanding condition, are loaded with "extras," enjoy views unavailable to other properties in the area, have a good location, or have other amenities uncommon for the area. Typical homes should not be penalized for the more pricey, uncommon characteristics of these homes.

The Proposed Solution
Eliminate the top 10 percent of all sale prices in a given area in assessors' calculations to determine the other appraised value of properties.

The Benefits
- Property owners of typical homes in an area would enjoy more fair and accurate appraisals.
- The number of protests will decrease as appraisal accuracy increases.

10. The Problem
Appraisal values are often inaccurate because the value of financing is not incorporated into appraisal calculations.

Why the Problem Needs to be Addressed

- Assessors do not deduct the value of financing from the sale prices, yet less than 10 percent of properties are cash sales.
- Sale price, less the value of personal property (as opposed to sale price less the value of personal property adjusted for a cash price), is used to determine the assessor's value on all property throughout the state for taxing purposes.
- Several types of financing serve to increase the sale price of the property. Examples include:

    Assumption transactions—A condominium sold for $60,000 by assumption alone often would sell for tens of thousands of dollars less if it were sold on a new loan (the new loan representing a truer value). Accounting for 14 percent of metropolitan properties sold, assumptions also usually mean significantly lower (often, $5,000—$10,000) closing costs. The value of the property is driven up by several additional factors, including:

    — Rarely is an appraisal done
    — The purchaser frequently does not need to qualify for the loan
    — The interest rate is often below the market value of mortgage money

    FHA and VA loans—These sales represent 49 percent of metropolitan property sales in today's market. The value of the property is driven up by several factors:

    — Almost all new FHA and VA-insured loan sales are transacted at below-market interest rates. As a result, thousands of dollars, called points, are paid to offset the interest rate loss to the bank.
    — The purchaser usually makes a downpayment of only 0-3 percent on the property.

    Owner-carry loans—When the seller carries any loan on behalf of the purchaser, the value of the property is driven up by several factors:

— Usually, no appraisal is done.

— A sizable reduction of closing costs, often totaling 5-8 percent of the loan amount, is common.

— Because the qualification process for the buyer is generally less stringent on owner-carry loans, the seller's risk of foreclosure increases. In addition, the seller can command a higher sale price for taking this risk.

Conventional loans—Properties sold with conventional loans (representing 25 percent of metropolitan property sales) usually command a sale price close to that of a cash sale. The interest rate is usually the same as, or close to, the value of mortgage money. Down payments are typically 10 percent or more of value.

The Proposed Solution

• Incorporate a simple set of discounts into the calculations to determine actual cash value at the time the assessor records the real estate transaction. All relevant data for the appraisal is already reported to the assessor (type of transaction, interest rate, points, down payment, etc.). Suggestions for the discounts include:

— Assumptions in which the buyer makes a 0-10 percent down payment: Disregard the sale price in determining values

— Assumptions in which the buyer makes more than a 10 percent down payment: Subtract 5 percent from the sale price

— VA and FHA-insured loans: Subtract 7 percent from the purchase price

— Owner-carry loans: Subtract 10 percent from the purchase price

— Conventional loans: Subtract two percent from the sale price

The Benefits

• Appraisals would be much more accurate and fair.
• Financing would be moved from the area of tax penalties to a level playing field.

11. The Problem
The current protest process often requires two protests and is handled inconsistently from one county to another.

Why the Problem Needs to be Addressed
- A property owner who successfully protests in 1991 receives a corrected valuation for 1992 as well. If a property owner who conducts a successful protest in 1992, when assessors have more time to review protests, the property owner must go to a certain amount of extra work and file for a refund in order to receive a correction for 1991.
- Currently, the assessor and/or county commissioners can even force a property owner who conducts a successful protest in the second year to go to another hearing, proving the same case, to obtain a refund for the first year.

The Proposed Solution
Offer an automatic tax credit for 1991 to property owners who conduct successful protests during 1992, when appropriate.

The Benefits
- Property owners would receive the refunds due them. In 1988, when legislators did allow automatic tax credits for 1987 to property owners who won their protests in 1988, property owners received refunds of over $32 million (see Appendix G).
- An automatic credit would eliminate needless paperwork, hassle, and effort from both the assessor and property owner to claim refunds. It would also mean less work for already overworked, understaffed county commissioner offices.

AFTERWORD

I have written *Overtaxed! Your Guide to Honest Property Tax Reductions by Understanding and Effectively Protesting Your Assessment* out of a sincere desire to help people in Colorado understand and reduce their property taxes. I set out to write the most comprehensive manual available on the subject, and believe I have succeeded. In writing it, I have withheld no information as my "special secret."

Growth is a never-ending process, so, as laws change yearly and more information becomes available, I will be updating the book appropriately. I would value any input from you, my readers, for these future editions and updates. I would also hope to add chapters on vacant land, agricultural, personal property taxes, as well as a special chapter on how to invest in property tax sales, in the future.

Let me know how the book has worked for you, what you found particularly helpful, and what information you found difficult to understand or use. Please let me know of your suggestions for improvement.

Although I can not guarantee you success, the methods outlined here have worked for tens of thousands of people who have used them in the past. Take your time, have fun, and pursue the money that belongs to you!

Appendix A

NUMBER OF PROTESTS: 1987, 1989

	1987	1989
Assessors *(first round)*		
Total parcels (pieces of property)	1,904,637	2,092,545
Parcels protested	220,176	175,234
Parcels protested as a percent of total parcels	11.56%	8.37%
County Boards of Equalization *(second round)*		
Parcels protested	27,544	*53,644
Parcels protested as a percent of assessor parcels protested	12.51%	30.61%
Board of Assessment Appeals *(third round)*		
Parcels protested	15,987	**11,106
Number of dockets	4,592	3,528

* Includes 21,759 for Costilla County, mostly vacant land

** Author's estimate

Source: Colorado Division of Property Taxation, Nineteenth Annual Report to the Governor

Appendix B

PROPERTY TAX REFUNDS FOR SELECTED COUNTIES 1989

REPORTED BY TREASURERS*

County	Tax Refunds**	Refunds Made	Average Amount
Adams	$302,101	497	$608
Arapahoe	11,770,143	1,885	6,244
Boulder	461,783	879	525
Denver	5,751,279	3,021	1,904
Douglas	441,883	1,221	362
Eagle	190,922	169	1,130
El Paso	993,745	983	1,011
Garfield	214,971	97	2,216
Grand	840,767	341	2,466
Gunnison	69,311	88	788
Jefferson	3,810,561	1,429	2,667
La Plata	51,512	208	248
Larimer	374,893	679	552
Logan	52,043	137	380
Mesa	350,803	431	814
Pueblo	392,130	915	429
Routt	179,068	85	2,107
Weld	314,093	977	321

Other Counties	520,239	2,125	295
Totals	$27,082,247	16,167	$1,675

* These refunds were paid in 1989 for prior-year appraisal errors. They are not dollar values for the reductions received at time of protest of property assessments

** Includes abatements, refunds, and collectables representing a very small percentage of the total.

Source: Compiled by the author from the Colorado Division of Property Taxation's Nineteenth Annual Report to the Governor

Appendix C

PROPERTY TAX REFUNDS FOR SELECTED COUNTIES 1988

REPORTED BY TREASURERS*

County	Tax Refunds**	Number of Refunds	Average Amount
Adams	$365,164	1,173	$311
Arapahoe	10,621,514	2,197	4,835
Archuleta	16,360	82	200
Boulder	679,205	446	1,523
Denver	6,945,766	2,996	2,318
Douglas	491,813	8,048	61
Eagle	247,269	217	1,139
El Paso	1,403,209	1,897	740
Fremont	87,489	276	317
Garfield	81,772	106	771
Grand	46,389	138	336
Gunnison	74,656	56	1,333
Jefferson	2,912,771	2,572	1,132
La Plata	124,270	134	927
Larimer	774,130	761	1,017
Logan	41,540	95	437
Mesa	277,685	615	452
Montezuma	16,544	74	224
Pueblo	98,787	204	484

Routt	252,101	120	2,101
Summitt	113,194	289	392
Weld	2,046,766	1,804	1,135
Other Counties	645,744	1,876	344
Totals	$28,364,088	$26,176	$1,084

* These refunds were paid in 1988 for prior-year appraisal errors. They are not dollar values for the reductions received at time of protest of property assessments.

** Includes abatements, refunds, and uncollectables, with uncollectables representing a very small percentage of the total.

Source: Compiled by the author from the Colorado Division of Property Taxation's Nineteenth Annual Report to the Governor

TOTAL REVENUE COLLECTED FROM PROPERTY TAXES

BY COUNTY—1989

COUNTY	*1989*
Adams	$156,093,528
Alamosa	4,998,687
Arapahoe	326,713,545
Archuletta	7,008,099
Baca	3,931,442
Bent	2,572,150
Boulder	160,364,398
Chaffee	5,227,040
Cheyenne	5,049,107
Clear Creek	8,241,449
Conejos	2,225,301
Costilla	3,970,586
Crowley	1,219,170
Custer	1,852,662
Delta	7,188,500
Denver	324,345,115
Dolores	1,301,690
Douglas	63,018,752
Eagle	37,251,463

Elbert	8,138,509
El Paso	202,438,214
Fremont	10,435,060
Garfield	19,325,398
Gilpin	3,084,136
Grand	16,237,579
Gunnison	9,244,096
Hinsdale	799,459
Huerfano	7,310,146
Jackson	1,267,895
Jefferson	284,135,177
Kiowa	2,667,833
Kit Carson	5,874,603
Lake	7,498,302
La Plata	21,347,997
Larimer	106,084,787
Las Animas	5,470,318
Lincoln	3,960,523
Logan	11,497,143
Mesa	42,218,474
Mineral	812,066
Moffat	18,204,275
Montezuma	12,037,184
Montrose	10,323,659
Morgan	17,744,358
Otero	5,147,358
Ouray	2,121,618
Park	7,340,799
Phillips	3,104,583
Pitkin	20,026,966
Prowers	6,016,625
Pueblo	53,104,102
Rio Blanco	14,014,881
Rio Grande	6,117,024
Routt	18,636,060
Saguache	3,064,138
San Juan	1,137,635
San Miguel	5,296,533
Sedgwick	2,367,967

Summit	24,351,387
Teller	9,203,029
Washington	5,327,358
Weld	86,399,520
Yuma	8,028,078
TOTAL	$2,231,535,538

Source: The Colorado Division of Property Taxation's Nineteenth Annual Report to the Governor

Appendix E

ESTIMATED APPRAISED ACTUAL VALUE OF COLORADO PROPERTY

BY CLASSIFICATION—1989
IN BILLIONS OF DOLLARS

Type	*Amount*	*Percent*
Residential	$87.43	61.56
Commercial	29.22	20.57
Industrial	5.65	3.98
Agricultural	2.21	1.56
Natural Resources	.65	.46
Producing Mines	.69	.49
Oil and Gas	1.11	.78
State Assessed*	7.61	5.36
Vacant Land	7.45	5.25
Total	$142.02	

* Includes public utility companies such as water, gas, telephone, airlines, pipelines, railroads, and private rail cars

Source: Colorado Public Expenditures Council Vol. XXXV. No. 8, June 15, 1989, via the Colorado Division of

Property Taxation, annual reports and 1989 Residential Rate Study

Note: Residential Divided by .15. All other classes divided by .29

ESTIMATED APPRAISED VALUE OF COLORADO EXEMPT PROPERTY

BY SUBCLASSES—1989
IN BILLIONS OF DOLLARS

Federal Government	$7.81
State of Colorado	2.18
Colorado Counties	1.44
Political Subdivisions*	3.86
Religious Worship	1.52
Private Schools	.53
Charitable Institutions	1.06
Parsonages, Etc.	.95
Miscellaneous	.37
Total Exempt	$20.08

* Special districts, i.e., Park and Recreation.

Note: Parsonages divided by .15. All other classes divided by .29

Source: Author, from Colorado Division of Property Taxation Nineteenth Annual Report to the Governor

Appendix F

COMMERCIAL PROPERTY TAX AGENTS

Name of Firm	Contact	Phone	Area Serviced
Bridge & Associates 870 Parfet Street, #700 Lakewood, CO	Greg Evans	(303) 237-6997	Front Range
Peter N. Ehrlich, P.C. 730 17th Street, #900 Denver, CO 80202	Peter Ehrlich	(303) 629-1007 (303) 629-1016	Front Range Summit Eagle Pitkin
William A. McLain, P.C. 300 Lincoln Street Denver, CO 80203	Bill McLain FAX	(303) 698-9595 (303) 698-9170	State of Colorado
Property Analysts, Ltd. 7675 W. 14th Ave., #105 Lakewood, CO 80215	Allen Major Charles Cook	(303) 234-1270	State of Colorado
Sterling Williams Group 23582 Pondview Place Golden, CO 80401	Steve Boblak	(303) 526-9665	State of Colorado

Appendix G

SPECIAL AUTOMATIC TAX CREDITS AND REFUNDS*
1988

REPORTED BY TREASURERS

COUNTY	TAX CREDITS & REFUNDS	NUMBER	AVERAGE REFUNDED
Adams	$817,819	657	$1,244
Arapahoe	5,935,721	5,010	1,185
Archuleta	518,276	5,464	95
Boulder	3,394,040	16,326	208
Denver	4,260,030	4,159	1,024
Douglas	1,062,061	5,085	209
Eagle	263,147	157	1,676
El Paso	1,806,508	1,269	1,424
Fremont	23,052	138	167
Garfield	**748,957	227	3,299
	***87,734	226	388
Grand	621,919	1,231	505
Gunnison	203,622	1,144	178
Jefferson	5,317,770	7,434	715
La Plata	155,812	254	613
Larimer	2,577,600	6,223	414
Logan	589,850	5,862	101
Mesa	1,777,758	4,003	444

Montezuma	104,188	334	312
Pueblo	192,421	512	376
Routt	262,503	849	309
Summit	92,064	213	432
Weld	1,103,290	7,406	149
Other Counties	563,038	2,116	266
TOTAL	**$32,391,440	76,083	**$426
	***$31,730,217	76,082	***$417

*   The Legislature made protest reductions received for 1988 tax
       bills automatic to property owners' 1987 tax bills, with certain
       limitations. This action was due to the 220,000 protests filed in
       the 1987 reappraisal, and the understanding that the assessment
       community and property owners needed to protest in 1988 to
       work through the problems of the 1987 reappraisal.

**   Includes Unocal's $661,223 refund.

***   Does not include Unocal's refund.

Source: Compiled by the author from the Colorado Division of Property
        Taxation's Nineteenth Annual Report to the Governor

Appendix H

BOARDS AND ASSOCIATIONS OF REALTORS

For help in finding a real estate appraiser, ask for a list of affiliate appraiser members.

Board/Association	City	Phone
METRO DISTRICT		
Aurora (association)	Aurora	(303) 369-5549
Denver (board)	Denver	(303) 756-0553
Douglas/Elbert (board)	Castle Rock	(303) 688-0941
Evergreen (board)	Evergreen	(303) 674-7020
Jefferson County (association)	Lakewood	(303) 233-7831
North Surburban (board)	Westminster	(303) 426-0662
South Surburban (board)	Littleton	(303) 797-3700
MOUNTAIN DISTRICT		
Aspen (board)	Aspen	(303) 925-5704
Grand County (board)	Granby	(303) 444-9461
Steamboat Springs (board)	Steamboat Springs	(303) 879-4663
Summit County (association)	Frisco	(303) 668-3624
Vail (board)	Vail	(303) 476-3598

NORTHEAST DISTRICT

Boulder (board)	Boulder	(303) 442-3585
Estes Park (board)	Estes Park	(303) 586-6628
Fort Collins (board)	Fort Collins	(303) 223-2900
Greeley (board)	Greeley	(303) 353-8884
Logan (board)	Sterling	(303) 522-8660
Longmont (association)	Longmont	(303) 772-5555
Loveland (board)	Loveland	(303) 669-1822
Morgan County (board)	Fort Morgan	(303) 867-2327

NORTHWEST DISTRICT

Colorado West (board)	Craig	(303) 824-4461
Delta County (board)	Delta	(303) 874-7501
Grand Junction (board)	Grand Junction	(303) 243-3322
Gunnison (board)	Crested Butte	(303) 641-3880
Montrose (board)	Montrose	(303) 249-7738
Upper Colorado (board)	Glenwood Springs	(303) 945-9762

SOUTHEAST DISTRICT

Arkansas Valley (board)	Rocky Ford	(719) 254-3587
Chaffee County (board)	Salida	(719) 539-4893
Pikes Peak (association)	Colorado Springs	(719) 633-7718
Fremont County (board)	Canon City	(719) 275-6560
Pueblo (board)	Pueblo	(719) 545-3666

SOUTHWEST DISTRICT

Archuleta County (board)	Pagosa Springs	(303) 264-4101
Four Corners (board)	Cortez	(303) 565-8939
La Plata (association)	Durango	Not Available
San Luis Valley (board)	Alamosa	(719) 589-2147
Telluride (board)	Telluride	(719) 728-5172

Appendix I

COUNTY ASSESSORS

County	Assessor	Phone
Adams	Pat Reale	(303) 659-2120, x157
Alamosa	Dorothy Yeater	(719) 589-3728
Arapahoe	Jim Reeves	(303) 795-4600
Archuletta	David Wilson	(303) 264-2826
Baca	Roscoe Hargrove	(719) 523-4332
Bent	Kitty Ann Long	(719) 456-2010
Boulder	Terry Phillips	(303) 441-3530/3527
Chaffee	Joann Boyd	(719) 539-4016
Cheyenne	Allen Petersen	(719) 767-5664
Clear Creek	Diane Settle	(303) 569-3251, x221
Conejos	David Martinez	(719) 376-5585
Costilla	Maclovio Martinez	(719) 672-3642
Crowley	Warren Davis	(719) 267-4421
Custer	J.D. Henrich	(719) 783-2218
Delta	Donna Ferganchick	(303) 874-3628
Denver	Larry Patterson	(303) 640-2211
Doloras	Pat Huskey	(303) 677-2385
Douglas	Ginger Chase	(303) 660-7450
Eagle	Cherlyn Baker	(303) 328-7311
Elbert	Karen Hart	(303) 621-2105
El Paso	Ted Shonts	(719) 520-6630/6605
Fremont	Jim Deatherage	(719) 275-1627
Garfield	Ken Call	(303) 945-9134
Gilpin	Glenda Allen	(303) 572-0567
Grand	Nancy Dakan Anders	(303) 725-3347, x217
Gunnison	Judy Smith	(303) 641-1085, x21
Hinsdale	Amy Wilcox	(303) 944-2224
Huerfano	Virginia Aragon	(719) 738-1191
Jackson	Jean Maxwell	(303) 723-4751

Jefferson	Judy Pettit	(303) 277-8300
Kiowa	Jimmy Bendorf	(719) 438-5521
Kit Carson	Juanita Davis	(719) 346-8946
Lake	Sandra Field	(719) 486-0413, x10
La Plata	Craig Larson	(303) 259-4000, x221
Larimer	Steve Miller	(303) 498-2050
Las Animas	Dan Espinoza	(719) 846-2295/2296
Lincoln	Estelle Thaller	(719) 743-2358
Logan	Jane Budin	(303) 522-2797
Mesa	James Farley	(303) 244-1610
Mineral	Robert Louth	(719) 658-2669
Moffat	Dennis Shanahan	(303) 824-8181
Montezuma	Robert N. Cruzan	(303) 565-3428
Montrose	Larry Pierce	(303) 249-3753
Morgan	Robert Wooldridge	(303) 867-2479
Otero	Marian Barnes	(719) 384-7921
Ouray	Donna French	(303) 325-4371
Park	Dave Wissel	(719) 836-2771
Phillips	Mary Belle Rafert	(303) 854-3151
Pitkin	Tom Issac	(303) 920-5160
Prowers	Andrew Wyatt	(719) 336-2209
Pueblo	Victor Plutt	(719) 546-6000
Rio Blanco	Renae Neilson	(303) 878-5686
Rio Grande	Robert Davie	(719) 657-3326
Routt	James W. Leary	(303) 879-2756
Saguache	Jacqueline Lujan-Bircher	(719) 655-2521
San Juan	Judy Zimmerman	(303) 387-5632
San Miguel	Peggy Kanter	(303) 728-3174
Sedgwick	Donna Carter	(303) 474-2531
Summit	Janeen Taylor	(303) 453-2561, x296
Teller	Reta Bowman	(719) 689-2941
Washington	Larry Griese	(303) 345-6662
Weld	Warren Lasell	(303) 356-4000
Yuma	Roberta Helling	(303) 332-5032

Appendix J

PETITION FOR ABATE-MENT OR REFUND OF TAXES FORM

15-DPT
FORM 920 1/66-6/90

FORM PRESCRIBED BY THE PROPERTY TAX ADMINISTRATOR
PETITION FOR ABATEMENT OR REFUND OF TAXES—c F HOECKEL CO. DENVER 36312

Petitioners: Use this side only.

.... , Colorado, .. , 19. ....
         City or Town

To The Honorable Board of County Commissioners of ... **County**

Gentlemen:

   The petition of.... .. . .

whose mailing address is: .. . .

.... City or Town . . .. .. State Zip Code

SCHEDULE NUMBER   **DESCRIPTION OF PROPERTY AS LISTED ON TAX ROLL**

respectfully requests that the taxes assessed against the above property for the years A. D. 19........., 19. , are erroneous, illegal, or due to error in valuation for the following reasons: **(Completely describe the circumstances surrounding the incorrect value or tax.)**

	19........ Value	Tax	19........ Value	Tax
Orig.				
Abate.				
Bal.				

The taxes (have) (have not) been paid. Wherefore your petitioner prays that the taxes may be abated or refunded in the sum of $. ....

I declare, under penalty of perjury in the second degree that this petition, together with any accompanying exhibits or statements, has been examined by me and to the best of my knowledge, information and belief is true, correct and complete.

....
                                          Petitioner

By........ ....
                                          Agent

Address.... ....

METRO DENVER RETAIL BUILDINGS 1989 PRICE PER SQUARE FOOT

Area	Number of Transactions	Price per Square Foot
Northwest Suburban		
Under 10,000 SF	16	$37.48
10,000 - 49,999 SF	3	48.71
50,000 & Up SF	2	50.50
Southwest Suburban		
Under 10,000 SF	4	43.37
10,000 - 49,999 SF	4	24.80
South Suburban		
Under 10,000 SF	5	35.91
10,000 - 49,999 SF	2	31.78
Southeast Denver & Suburban		
Under 10,000 SF	7	23.12
10,000 - 49,999 SF	2	40.00
50,000 & Up SF	3	50.85
South Denver		
Under 10,000 SF	11	30.66
10,000 - 49,999 SF	2	19.68

Midtown

Under 10,000 SF	5	24.69
10,000 - 49,999 SF	7	51.64

North Denver & Suburban

Under 10,000 SF	4	31.87
10,000 - 49,999 SF	5	46.52
50,000 & Up SF	2	28.69

Northeast Denver & Suburban

Under 10,000 SF	6	20.02
10,000 - 49,999 SF	2	22.68

Overall Price per Square Foot in Each Area

Northwest Suburban	21	46.11
Southwest Suburban	8	18.25
South Suburban	8	39.09
Southeast Denver & Suburban	12	47.29
South Denver	13	24.75
Midtown	32	36.50
North Denver & Suburban	11	34.68
Northeast Denver & Suburban	8	22.24

Metro Denver Retail Building Sales by Size

Under 10,000 SF	68	32.50
10,000 - 19,000 SF	22	30.17
20,000 - 49,999 SF	11	44.96
50,000 - 99,999 SF	7	29.65
100,000 & Up SF	5	41.42

Metro Denver Retail Building Sales by Age

Before 1950	36	25.21
1950-1959	14	19.40
1960-1969	25	36.77
1970-1979	20	27.86
1980-1989	18	46.64

Note: Data contains arms-length transactions, without age taken into consideration.

Source: Information compiled by author with permission of Dresco, from their Roddy Reports' valuation guide

METRO DENVER INDUSTRIAL WAREHOUSE BUILDINGS 1989 PRICE PER SQUARE FOOT

Area	Number Of Transactions	Price per Square Foot
Northwest Suburban		
Under 20,000 SF	5	$29.47
Southeast Denver & Suburban		
Under 20,000 SF	6	27.40
South Denver		
Under 20,000 SF	15	23.83
20,000 - 69,999 SF	4	23.10
70,000 & Up SF	3	17.01
Midtown		
Under 20,000 SF	26	25.07
20,000 - 69,999 SF	9	15.97
70,000 & Up SF	2	11.93
North Denver & Suburban		
Under 20,000 SF	20	28.06
20,000 - 69,999 SF	11	23.31
70,000 & Up SF	7	18.47

Northeast Denver and Suburban		
Under 20,000 SF	15	27.91
20,000 - 69,999 SF	6	18.99
70,000 & Up SF	9	19.04

Note: Data contains arms-length transactions, without age taken into consideration.

Source: Information compiled by author with permission of Dresco, from their Roddy Reports' valuation guide

Appendix M

METRO DENVER OFFICE BUILDINGS 1989 PRICE PER SQUARE FOOT

Area	Number of Transactions	Price per Square Foot
Northwest Suburban		
Under 10,000 SF	9	$38.11
10,000 - 49,999 SF	3	28.32
Southwest Suburban		
Under 10,000 SF	7	41.20
10,000 - 49,999 SF	6	41.56
50,000 & Up SF	4	37.16
South Suburban		
Under 10,000 SF	6	30.93
10,000 - 49,999 SF	4	26.44
Southeast		
Under 10,000 SF	9	58.08
10,000 - 49,999 SF	14	37.92
50,000 & Up SF	12	46.00
South Denver		
Under 10,000 SF	7	58.33
Midtown (not including Cherry Creek or Central Business District)		
Under 10,000 SF	23	27.78
10,000 - 49,999 SF	5	26.45

North Denver & Suburban		
Under 10,000 SF	6	52.37
10,000 - 49,999 SF	4	40.86
Northeast Denver & Suburban		
Under 10,000 SF	6	36.06

Office Building Transaction Overall Average

Southwest Suburban Area	17	38.21
South Suburban Area	11	38.82
Southeast Denver & Suburban Area	35	44.85
South Denver Area	10	30.75
Midtown Area	31	33.31
Cherry Creek Area	5	69.91
North Denver & Suburban Area	11	39.32
Northeast Denver & Suburban Area	7	27.28

Note: Data contains arms-length transactions, without age taken into consideration.

Source: Information compiled by author with permission of Dresco, from their Roddy Reports' valuation guide

Appendix N

METRO DENVER LAND 1989 PRICE PER SQUARE FOOT

Area	Number of Transactions	Price per Square Foot
Commercial		
Northwest Suburban	16	$5.45
North Suburban	6	3.00
Northeast Denver & Suburban	6	3.02
Industrial		
Northwest Suburban	6	2.33
Northeast Denver & Suburban	17	1.51
Under 5 acres		
Over 5 acres	5	.66
North Denver	17	1.52
South Suburban	8	2.03
Southeast Suburban	4	1.77
PUD (Planned Unit Development)/Mixed Use		
Northwest Suburban	9	.89
North Suburban		
Under 20 acres	3	1.07
Over 20 acres	4	.42
Northeast Denver & Suburban	11	.73

Note: Data contains arms-length transactions, without location
          taken into consideration, and usually without size taken into
          consideration.

Source: Information compiled by author with permission of Dresco,
          from their Roddy Reports' valuation guide

Appendix O

REAL PROPERTY TRANSFER DECLARATION FORM

Attorneys, Realtors, title company personnel, and property buyers should use care when utilizing the "Real Property Transfer Declaration" form, required at all real estate closings since July 1, 1988, as a properly completed form can serve to *reduce* the valuation of a property for tax purposes.

Specifically, Questions 2 and 5 alert the assessor to refrain from using the sale price of the property in the calculations to determine the appraisal value of that property or other properties similar to it. These questions seek to identify transactions in which the sale price is artificially high or low —often the case when properties are sold to family members. "Related parties" also refers to close business associates.

Question 6 refers to (c) above. The value you place here reduces the assessor's valuation of your property as well as others similar to it. For example, if the property sold for $100,000, and included $3,000 in personal property (such as wall-to-wall or unattached carpeting, window coverings, free-standing appliances, inventory, equipment, furniture, sheds, goodwill, water, or mineral rights, etc.), then the assessor would adjust its value to $97,000. Note that personal property is usually, but not always, unattached to the property.

In the case of apartments and commercial/industrial property, the correct information provided in Question 6 also helps to eliminate double taxation, as these same items would also be taxed on a personal property tax schedule. For example, fixtures, as well as the desks, typewriters, and machinery in an industrial building are all taxed annually, just like a house. Residential properties, with the exception of apartment buildings, by law, are *not* subject to personal property taxes.

Most people believe that the purpose of Question 6 is to identify personal property in residential homes so that it can be taxed, just like commercial personal property is taxed. This is simply not true. Unfortunately, however, many people are not answering Question 6, thereby hurting property tax positions.

In addition, many people are not aware that wall-to-wall carpeting, even though it is attached, *is* considered personal property in the eyes of the assessor.

Question 7 applies to commercial and industrial property. If the transaction included commercial or industrial property, make sure to note that here, along with its value—even if you have already done so on a separate form or bill of sale. The same requirements apply to water rights for all types of property (residential, agricultural, commercial/industrial).

Question 9 applies to commercial and industrial properties. Make sure you fill this in accurately, as it will reduce your valuation dollar for dollar.

Questions 4 and 12-15 currently are being used only to identify unusual or special financing transactions so that an appropriate sale price adjustment can be made for valuation purposes.

If you have already filled out the form, but think you have made an error, or if you left any question unanswered, let your assessor know. You can go back and change/update the form at any time.

REAL PROPERTY TRANSFER DECLARATION

1. Address or legal description of real property: _____

   _____

2. Is this transaction between related parties? Yes ☐ No ☐

3. Total sale price: $ _____

4. What was the cash down payment? $ _____

5. Did total sale price include a trade or exchange?
   Yes ☐ No ☐

6. Did the buyer receive any personal property in the transaction? Yes ☐ No ☐
   If yes, the approximate value: $ _____

7. Were mineral rights included in the sale? Yes ☐ No ☐

8. Were water rights included in the sale? Yes ☐ No ☐

9. If applicable, you may include goodwill for a going business. Approximate value of goodwill? $ _____

10. Was less than 100% interest in the real property conveyed?
    Yes ☐ No ☐

11. Date of closing: _____
                                 month   year

12. Was the loan new ☐ or assumed ☐?

13. What was the interest rate on the loan? _____

14. What was the term of the loan? _____

15. Were any points paid? Yes ☐ No ☐
    If yes, how many? _____

16. Signed this _____ day of _____ , 19 __

    ☐ Grantor ☐ Grantee _____

    ☐ Grantor ☐ Grantee _____

Appendix P

METRO DENVER APARTMENT BUILDING 1989 PRICE PER UNIT

Area	Number of Transactions	Sales Price per Unit
Northwest Suburban		
8-24 Units	9	$18,714
Southwest Suburban		
25-74 Units	5	19,115
Southeast Denver & Suburban		
8-24 Units	5	11,759
25-74 Units	7	14,805
South Denver		
8-24 Units	6	21,314
25-74 Units	3	11,911
Midtown		
8-24 Units	39	14,119
25-74 Units	14	13,427
Northeast Denver & Suburban		
8-24 Units	17	10,591
25-74 Units	7	9,227

AVERAGE PRICE PER UNIT BY AREA
ON ALL SALES 8 UNITS & LARGER

Northwest Suburban	12	$17,645
Southwest Suburban	9	19,483
South Suburban	4	20,230
Southeast Denver & Suburban	13	14,963
South Denver	9	15,894
Midtown	54	12,970
North Denver	5	12,653
Northeast Denver & Suburban	27	9,885

Note: Data contains arms-length transactions, without age taken into consideration.

Source: Information compiled by author with permission of Dresco, from their Roddy Reports' valuation guide

Appendix Q

APARTMENT RENTS PER SQUARE FOOT BY COUNTY AND TYPE*

SECOND QUARTER 1990

TYPE OF APARTMENTS	*AVERAGE MONTHLY RENT PER SQUARE FOOT*
ADAMS COUNTY	
Efficiency	$.50
1 Bedroom	.53
2 Bedroom/1 Bath	.47
2 Bedroom/2 Bath	.49
3 Bedroom	.44
All	.50
ARAPAHOE COUNTY	
Efficiency	.51
1 Bedroom	.51
2 Bedroom/1 Bath	.47
2 Bedroom/2 Bath	.51
3 Bedroom	.45
All	.50
BOULDER COUNTY	
Efficiency	.78
1 Bedroom	.67
2 Bedroom/1 Bath	.55
2 Bedroom/2 Bath	.57
3 Bedroom	.50
All	.60

DENVER COUNTY

Efficiency	.51
1 Bedroom	.52
2 Bedroom/1 Bath	.48
2 Bedroom/2 Bath	.51
3 Bedroom	.38
All	.50

DOUGLAS COUNTY

1 Bedroom	.58
2 Bedroom/1 Bath	.47
2 Bedroom/2 Bath	.50
All	.50

JEFFERSON COUNTY

Efficiency	.54
1 Bedroom	.55
2 Bedroom/1 Bath	.47
2 Bedroom/2 Bath	.49
3 Bedroom	.45
All	.50

* Rents are based on the units being unfurnished with tenants paying electricity and gas.

Average rents do not reflect "rental losses" from discounts/concessions, models, deliquents, and bad debts.

Average rent minus rental loss equals effective rent.

Source: Reprinted with permission of the University of Denver and the Apartment Association of Metro Denver. From the *Denver Area Apartment Vacancy Survey,* Second Quarter 1990, Gordon E. Von Stroh, Ph.D., Graduate School of Business and Public Management, College of Business Administration at the University of Denver.

Appendix R

AVERAGE APARTMENT RENTS BY COUNTY AND SIZE OF BUILDING*

SECOND QUARTER 1990

NUMBER OF APARTMENTS	MONTHLY RENT PER UNIT
ADAMS COUNTY	
2 - 8	$355.05
9 - 50	303.29
51 - 99	332.90
100 - up	382.45
ARAPAHOE COUNTY	
2 - 8	395.63
9 - 50	332.38
51 - 99	344.82
100 - up	404.88
BOULDER COUNTY	
2 - 8	628.54
9 - 50	468.74
51 - 99	401.06
100 - up	459.62
DENVER COUNTY	
2 - 8	310.52
9 - 50	280.46
51 - 99	421.90
100 - up	425.54

DOUGLAS COUNTY

2 - 8	263.00
9 - 50	580.00
51 - 99	387.35

JEFERSON COUNTY

2 - 8	368.93
9 - 50	387.29
51 - 99	405.34
100 - up	415.54

* Rents are based on the units being unfurnished with tenants paying electricity and gas.

Average rents do not reflect "rental losses" from discounts/concessions, models, delinquents, and bad debts.

Average rent minus rental loss equals effective rent.

Source: Reprinted with permission of the University of Denver and the Apartment Association of Metro Denver. From the *Denver Area Apartment Vacancy Survey,* Second Quarter 1990, Gordon E. Von Stroh, Ph.D., Graduate School of Business and Public Management, College of Business Administration at the University of Denver.

Appendix S

AVERAGE APARTMENT RENTS BY COUNTY AND AGE OF BUILDING*

SECOND QUARTER 1990

APARTMENT AGE	MONTHLY RENT PER UNIT
ADAMS COUNTY	
To 1959	$290.78
1960 - 1969	319.72
1970 - 1979	329.77
1980 -	432.62
ARAPAHOE COUNTY	
To 1959	231.33
1960 - 1969	311.99
1970 - 1979	332.40
1980 -	444.43
BOULDER COUNTY	
To 1959	553.17
1960 - 1969	394.93
1970 - 1979	490.39
1980 -	544.17
DENVER COUNTY	
To 1959	321.79
1960 - 1969	353.77
1970 - 1979	392.61
1980 -	522.04

DOUGLAS COUNTY
To 1959	263.00
1960 - 1969	
1970 - 1979	355.09
1980 -	421.33

JEFFERSON COUNTY
To 1959	294.29
1960 - 1969	352.74
1970 - 1979	383.27
1980 -	472.90

*   Rents are based on the units being unfurnished with tenants paying electricity and gas.

Average rents do not reflect "rental losses" from discounts/concessions, models, delinquents, and bad debts.

Source: Reprinted with permission of the University of Denver and the Apartment Association of Metro Denver. From the *Denver Area Apartment Vacancy Survey,* Second Quarter 1990, Gordon E. Von Stroh, Ph.D., Graduate School of Business and Public Management, College of Business Administration at the University of Denver.

Appendix T

AVERAGE APARTMENT RENTS BY COUNTY AND TYPE*

SECOND QUARTER 1990

APARTMENT TYPE	MONTHLY RENT PER UNIT
ADAMS COUNTY	
Efficiency	$245.25
1 Bedroom	324.57
2 Bedroom/1 Bath	382.78
2 Bedroom/2 Bath	460.34
3 Bedroom	458.15
All	363.97
ARAPAHOE COUNTY	
Efficiency	240.90
1 Bedroom	329.98
2 Bedroom/1 Bath	408.84
2 Bedroom/2 Bath	492.32
3 Bedroom	604.60
All	389.54
BOULDER COUNTY	
Efficiency	333.85
1 Bedroom	392.82
2 Bedroom/1 Bath	457.16
2 Bedroom/2 Bath	555.99
3 Bedroom	622.30
All	460.03

DENVER COUNTY   227.02
Efficiency   342.29
1 Bedroom   422.87
2 Bedroom/1 Bath   537.91
2 Bedroom/2 Bath   486.70
3 Bedroom   392.52
All

DOUGLAS COUNTY   464.37
2 Bedroom/1 Bath   354.05
2 Bedroom/2 Bath   463.00
3 Bedroom   417.49
All

JEFFERSON COUNTY   251.89
Efficiency   367.54
1 Bedroom   404.26
2 Bedroom/1 Bath   476.46
2 Bedroom/2 Bath   507.53
3 Bedroom   409.35
All

* Rents are based on the units being unfurnished with tenants paying electricity and gas.

  Average rents do not reflect "rental losses" from discounts/concessions, models, delinquents, and bad debts.

  Average rent minus rental loss equals effective rent.

Source: Reprinted with permission of the University of Denver and the Apartment Association of Metro Denver. From the *Denver Area Apartment Vacancy Survey,* Second Quarter 1990, Gordon E. Von Stroh, Ph.D., Graduate School of Business and Public Management, College of Business Administration at the University of Denver.

Appendix U

APARTMENT VACANCIES BY SIZE OF BUILDING

SECOND QUARTER 1990

SIZE OF BUILDING	YEARLY PERCENTAGE VACANCY RATE
ADAMS COUNTY	
2 - 8	27.3
9 - 50	13.0
51 - 99	18.9
100 - up	8.4
ARAPAHOE COUNTY	
2 - 8	21.1
9 - 50	10.6
51 - 99	13.4
100 - up	10.1
BOULDER COUNTY	
2 - 8	3.1
9 - 50	12.6
51 - 99	16.7
100 - up	9.9
DENVER COUNTY	
2 - 8	6.9
9 - 50	13.5
51 - 99	9.9
100 - up	8.6

DOUGLAS COUNTY
9 - 50	2.5
51 - 99	2.7

JEFERSON COUNTY
2 - 8	8.4
9 - 50	7.6
51 - 99	9.0
100 - up	5.7

Source: Reprinted with permission of the University of Denver and the Apartment Association of Metro Denver. From the *Denver Area Apartment Vacancy Survey*, Second Quarter 1990, Gordon E. Von Stroh, Ph.D., Graduate School of Business and Public Management, College of Business Administration at the University of Denver.

Appendix V

APARTMENT VACANCIES BY COUNTY AND AGE OF BUILDING

SECOND QUARTER 1990

APARTMENT AGE	PERCENTAGE VACANCY RATE
ADAMS COUNTY	
1960 - 1969	10.1
1970 - 1979	11.2
1980 -	6.1
ARAPAHOE COUNTY	
1950 - 1959	29.0
1960 - 1969	17.5
1970 - 1979	18.1
1980 -	7.0
BOULDER COUNTY	
1960 - 1969	6.8
1970 - 1979	12.2
1980 -	5.0
DENVER COUNTY	
To 1939	17.4
1940 - 1949	5.4
1950 - 1959	9.0
1960 - 1969	13.6
1970 - 1979	10.9
1980 -	4.4

DOUGLAS COUNTY
1970 - 1979   5.1

JEFFERSON COUNTY
1950 - 1959   10.1
1960 - 1969   8.7
1970 - 1979   7.6
1980 -   4.0

Source: Reprinted with permission of the University of Denver and
        the Apartment Association of Metro Denver. From the
        Denver Area Apartment Vacancy Survey, Second Quarter
        1990, Gordon E. Von Stroh, Ph.D., Graduate School of
        Business and Public Management, College of Business
        Administration at the University of Denver.

METRO DENVER COMMERCIAL OFFICE SPACE VACANCY RATES AND RENTAL INCOME

JUNE 30, 1990

	# OF BUILDINGS	PERCENT VACANCY RATE	RENTAL INCOME RANGE*	RENTAL INCOME
Central Business District	134	21.60	$5-$20	$10.64
Cherry Creek/Southeast	144	26.50	4-18	10.30
Denver Tech Center	58	16.80	7-17	12.25
Mid Town	81	19.80	5-14	8.70
Inverness	26	26.60	8.5-13.25	10.34
Union Sqaure/Southwest	134	24.30	5-12.5	9.22
Aurora	83	25.30	5-13	9.73
Northwest	130	21.80	5.5-15	10.58

Greenwood Plaza	56	24.40	5-17	11.76
Southeast Sub. Other	71	29.70	5-14	9.18
Northeast	24	40.70	5-12	8.22
TOTALS	941	23.10	4-20	10.27

* Monthly average per square foot rate (rentable)

Source: The Denver Metro Building Owners and Managers Association (B.O.M.A.)

Appendix X

METRO DENVER RETAIL SPACE VACANCY RATES

JUNE 30, 1990

	PERCENT VACANCY RATE
Central Business District	13.96
Cherry Creek/Southeast	5.46
Denver Tech Center	16.09
Mid Town	17.44
Inverness	16.78
Union Square/Southwest	16.11
Aurora	19.37
Northwest	16.00
Greenwood Plaza	19.37
Southeast Sub. Other	17.29
Northeast	23.98
TOTALS	16.91

Source: The Denver Metro Building Owners and Managers Association (B.O.M.A.)

METRO DENVER RETAIL SPACE VACANCY RATES

Appendix Y

REQUEST TO COMBINE PROPERTIES FORM

Please list the tax districts and schedule numbers of the properties you wish to combine.

_____

_____

Please answer the following questions:
1. Do any of the above schedule numbers have tax liens or unpaid taxes for prior years? _____

   _____

2. Is the land being combined considered a building site?
   Yes   No ☐

3. If the land is not a building site, explain why: _____

   _____

4. How many building sites are involved? _____

5. Is the land being combined with vacant land?
   Yes ☐ No ☐

This form must be completed before combinations can be processed.

Owner's Signature _____

Date _____

Mailing Address _____

Phone _____

Appendix Z

COUNTY TREASURERS AND COUNTY COMMISSIONERS

T = Treasurer   C = Commissioner   B = Board of Equalization

County	Treasurer	Commissioners	Phone
Adams	Helen Hill	Elaine Valente	T (303) 659-2120
		Jim Nelms	C (303) 659-2120
		Harold Kite	B (303) 659-2120
Alamosa	Chalene Cockrum	Robert Zimmerman	T (719) 589-3626
		Jim Jones	C (719) 589-3841
		Tim Gallagher	B (719) 589-3841
Arapahoe	Dorothy Vogt	Bob Brooks	T (303) 795-4550
		Thomas Eggert	C (303) 795-4360
		Jeanne Jolly	B (303) 795-4360
		John Nichol	
Archuletta	Traves Garrett	Mamie Lynch	T (303) 264-2152
		Jerry Martinez	C (303) 264-2536
		J. Robert Formwalt	B (303) 264-2536
Baca	Vira Forrest	Don Self	T (719) 523-4262
		Roy Brinkley	C (719) 523-6532
		Ray Miller	B (719) 523-6532
		Robert Chenoweth	
Bent	Alta Mae Brown	Harrell Ridley	T (719) 456-4211
		Gerald Faust	C (719) 456-1600
		Ralph Tixier	B (719) 456-1600
Boulder	George Forsyth	Sandy Hume	T (303) 441-3520
		Ronald Stewart	C (303) 441-3500
		Homer Page	B (303) 441-3500

Chaffee	Sandra Wilkins	John McFarland	T (719) 539-6808
		Terry Barkett	C (719) 539-2218
		Tom M. Eve	B (719) 539-2218
Cheyenne	Marlene	Floyd McEwen	T (719) 767-5657
	Schmeckpeper	Morgan Buck	C (719) 767-5872
		Karl Huenergardt	B (719) 767-5872
Clear Creek	Geraldine Thompson	Nelson Fugate	T (303) 569-3251
		Peter Kenney	C (303) 569-3251
		George Dickinson	B (303) 569-3251
Conejos	Mark Crowther	Johnnie Marquez	T (303) 376-5585
		Avelino Muniz	C (303) 376-5585
		Miguel DeHerrera	B (303) 376-5585
Costilla	Cosme Sanchez, Jr.	George Valdez	T (719) 672-3342
		Ernest Chavez	C (719) 672-3372
		Fred Sanchez	B (719) 672-3372
Crowley	Lynne Bauer	Robert Johnson	T (719) 267-4624
		Blaine Arbuthnot	C (719) 267-4643
		Jim McCleary	B (719) 267-4643
Custer	Doris Porth	John Coleman	T (719) 783-2341
		George Draper	C (719) 783-2259
		Robert Senderhauf	B (719) 783-2259
Delta	Mildred Hamilton	Jim Ventrello	T (303) 874-4449
		Bob Watson	C (303) 874-7589
		Ted Hayden	B (719) 874-7595
Denver	Alan Charnes	Alan Charnes	T (303) 640-2262
		Felicia Muftic	C (303) 640-2561
		William Roberts	B (303) 640-2561
		Paul Hack	
		Paul Hoskins	
Dolores	Shirley Hasty	Louis Bucher	T (719) 677-2386
		Wayne Twilley	C (719) 677-2383
		Myron Jones	B (719) 677-2383
		Orville Jahnke	
Douglas	Marilyn Green	James Sullivan	T (303) 660-7417
		Susan McDanal	C (303) 660-7400
		Chris Christensen	B (303) 660-7400
Eagle	Sherry Branden	Donald Welch	T (303) 328-7311
		Richard Gustafson	C (303) 328-7311
		Bud Gates	B (303) 328-7311
Elbert	Suzie Graeff	Robert Hall	T (719) 621-2104
		David Wright	C (719) 621-2348
		Frank Starkey	B (719) 621-2348
El Paso	Sharon Shipley	Marcy Morrison	T (719) 520-6666
		Jim Campbell	C (719) 520-6444
		Loren Whittmore	B (719) 520-6430
		Jeri Howells	
		Gary Shupp	
Fremont	Virginia Woltemath	Jim Griffin	T (719) 275-1521
		Charles McCall	C (719) 275-1515
		Bud Chess	B (719) 275-1515

Garfield	Georgia Chamberlain	Marian Smith	T (303) 945-9134
		Buckey Arbaney	C (303) 945-9134
		Arnold Mackley	B (303) 945-9134
Gilpin	Virginia Lee Starkey	Carroll Beck	T (303) 572-0567
		Leslie Williams	C (303) 572-0567
		Ann Lessingwell	B (303) 572-0567
		James Collin	
Grand	Margaret Alt	Richard Leonard	T (303) 725-3347
		Jerry Woods	C (303) 725-3347
		Paul Ohri	B (303) 725-3347
Gunnison	Alva May Dunbar	J.A. Santareli	T (303) 641-2231
		Fred Field	C (303) 641-0248
		Mario Petri	B (303) 641-0248
Hinsdale	Verna Carl	James Lewis	T (303) 944-2223
		Hubert Laird	C (303) 944-2225
		Ed Toner	B (303) 944-2225
Huerfano	Shirley Zubal	William Reiners	T (719) 738-1191
		Xavier Sandoval	C (719) 738-2370
		Neil Cocco	B (719) 738-2370
Jackson	Mildred Jill Potter	Robert Carlstrom	T (303) 723-4220
		Dennis Brinker	C (303) 723-4660
		Anthony Martin	B (303) 723-4660
Jefferson	Thomas McTurk	John Stone	T (303) 277-8553
		Marjorie Clement	C (303) 277-8505
		Rich Ferdinandsen	B (303) 277-8797
Kiowa	Steve Baxter	Burl Scherler	T (719) 438-5831
		Cardon Berry	C (719) 438-5810
		Leonard Price	B (719) 438-5810
Kit Carson	Sandra Berry	Dean Stevens	T (719) 346-8434
		Edgar Pratt	C (719) 346-8638
		Larry Herndon	B (719) 346-8638
Lake	Janice Fairchild	Edward O'Leary	T (719) 486-0530
		Donald Moffett	C (719) 486-0993
		John Saunders	B (719) 486-0993
La Plata	Edward Murray	Doris Brennan	T (303) 249-4000
		Fred Klatt	C (303) 249-4000
		Paul Brown	B (303) 249-4000
Larimer	Chuck Woodward	Courtlyn Hotchkiss	T (303) 221-7030
		Moe Mekelburg	C (303) 221-7010
		Daryle Klassen	B (303) 221-7010
Las Animas	Anthony Abeyta	Eugene Lujan	T (719) 846-2981
		James Healey	C (719) 846-3481
		Ken Clark	B (719) 846-3481
Lincoln	James Covington	Russell Covington	T (719) 743-2633
		Donald Weaver	C (719) 743-2444
		Harvey Wann	B (719) 743-2444
Logan	Barbara Kaiser	Bernard McLavey	T (303) 522-2462
		Don Korrey	C (303) 522-2462
		Jerry Montague	B (303) 522-2462

Mesa	Gena Harrison	Doralyn Genova	T (303) 244-1833
		John Leane	C (303) 522-2462
		Jim Spehar	B (303) 522-2462
Mineral	Dick Kolisch	Rod Wintz	T (719) 658-2325
		Gordon Hosselkus	C (719) 658-2360
		Robert Boppe	B (719) 658-2360
Moffat	Joy Hammat	Dean Visintainer	T (303) 824-6670
		Thomas LeFevre	C (303) 824-5517
		Thomas Mathers	B (303) 824-5517
Montezuma	Bobbie Spore	Robert Brubaker	T (303) 565-7550
		Thomas Colbert	C (303) 565-8317
		Robert Maynes	B (303) 565-8317
Montrose	Herbert Anderson	Arthur Schmalz	T (303) 249-3565
		Cindy Bowen	C (303) 249-7755
		Mel Staats	B (303) 249-7755
		Walt Burke	
Morgan	Robert Sagel	Bruce Bass	T (303) 867-8524
		Richard Neb	C (303) 867-8202
		Cynthia Erker	B (303) 867-8202
Otero	Dennis Smith	Robert Bauserman	T (719) 384-5473
		Bob Gerler	C (719) 384-7785
		Jack Klein	B (719) 384-7785
Ouray	Ramona Radcliff	Don Caddy	T (303) 325-4487
		Howard Williams	C (303) 325-4961
		Donald Sayers	B (303) 325-4961
Park	Vickie Roberts	Patricia Montgomery	T (719) 836-2771
		James Coggin, Jr.	C (719) 836-2771
		Glenn New	B (719) 836-2771
Phillips	Linda Statz	Tommy Thompson	T (303) 854-2882
		Larry Haynes	C (303) 854-2454
		Jay Martin	B (303) 854-2454
Pitkin	Tom Oken	Fred Crowley	T (303) 920-5170
		Hershall Ross	C (303) 920-5150
		Jim True	B (303) 920-5150
		Bill Tuite	
Prowers	Clara Weber	Joe Hasser	T (719) 336-2081
		Darrell Seufer	C (719) 336-9001
		Bob Tempel	B (719) 336-9001
Pueblo	Aureilo Sisneros	James Brewer	T (719) 546-6000
		Sollie Rasso	C (719) 546-6000
		Kathy Farley	B (719) 546-6000
Rio Blanco	Joann Findlay	Don Davis	T (719) 878-3614
		Joe Collins	C (719) 878-5001
		David Smith	B (719) 878-5001
Rio Grande	Billie Jean Garretson	Vern Rominger	T (719) 657-2747
		Robert Schaefer	C (719) 657-2744
		Meloin Getz	B (719) 657-2744
Routt	Kenneth Sigley	Dennis Fisher	T (303) 879-1732
		Robert Dorr	C (303) 879-0108
		Randolph Taylor	B (303) 879-0108

Saguache	Gladys Hazard	Chuck Grant	T (719) 655-2656
		Keith Edwards	C (719) 655-2231
		James Hines	B (719) 655-2231
San Juan	Beverly Eileen	Ernie Kuhlman	T (303) 387-5448
		Richard Perino	C (303) 387-5635
		Philip Dalla Antonelli II	B (303) 387-5635
San Miguel	Sherry Rose	Jim Bedford	T (303) 728-4451
		Carmen Lawrence	C (303) 728-3844
		Bill Wenger	B (303) 728-3844
Sedgwick	Ruth Schweitzer	Clark Bernhardt	T (719) 474-3346
		Chuck Powell	C (719) 474-2485
		Raymond Anderson	B (719) 474-2485
Summit	Larry Gilliland	Marsha Osborn Joseph Sands	T (303) 453-2561 x207
		Rick Hum	C (303) 453-2561 x334
			B (303) 453-2561 x334
Teller	Gaynell Holcomb	Robert Bergman	T (719) 689-2985
		LeMoyne Browning	C (719) 689-2988
		Frank Ricard	B (719) 689-2988
Washington	Marijane Keim	Paul Florian	T (303) 345-6601
		Elton Brown	C (303) 345-2701
		John Howlett	B (303) 345-2701
Weld	Francis Loustalet	Bill Kirby	T (303) 356-4000
		Gordon Lacy	C (303) 356-4000
		George Kennedy Bill Webster Connie Harbert	B (303) 356-4000
Yuma	Mary Lou Rose	Stanley Shafer	T (303) 332-4965
		David Frank	C (303) 332-5796
			B (303) 332-5796

Appendix AA

CITIES/TOWNS OFFERING PROPERTY TAX CREDITS/DEFERRALS FOR SENIORS

Arvada
Aspen
Boulder
Commerce City
Denver
Edgewater
Fort Collins
Greeley
Littleton
Longmont
Louisville
Nederland
Thornton

Source: Colorado Municipal League, *Municipal Taxes*, 1988 Edition

Appendix BB

COLORADO DAILY AND WEEKLY NEWSPAPERS

AKRON
Akron News-Reporter   69 Main Street, Akron, CO 80720

ALAMOSA
Valley Courier   401 State Ave., Alamosa, CO 81101

ARVADA
Arvada Sentinel   5801 W. 44th Ave., Unit L-1, Denver, CO 80212

ASPEN
Aspen Times   310 E. Main St., Aspen, CO 81611

AURORA
Aurora Sentinel   5801 W. 44th Ave. Unit L-1 Denver, CO 80212

BAYFIELD
Pine River Times   15 W. Mill Blvd., Bayfield, CO 81122

BERTHOUD
The Old Berthoud Recorder   344 Mountain Ave., Berthoud, CO 80513

BOULDER
Daily Camera   1048 Pearl, Boulder, CO 80302

BRECKENRIDGE
Summit County Journal   612 S. Ridge St., C, Breckenridge, CO 80424

BRIGHTON
Brighton Standard-Blade   139 N. Main St., Brighton, CO 80601

BRUSH
Brush News-Tribune   109 Clayton, Brush, CO 80723

BUENA VISTA
Chaffee County Times   101 Centennial Place, Buena Vista, CO
                                    81211

BURLINGTON
The Burlington Record   202 14th Street, Burlington, CO 80807

CANON CITY
Daily Record   523 Main, Canon City, CO 81212

CARBONDALE
The Valley Journal   358 Main Street, Carbondale, CO 81623

CASTLE ROCK
Daily News-Press   319 Perry St., Castle Rock, CO 80104

CENTER
Center Post-Dispatch   304 Worth, Center, CO 81125

CENTRAL CITY
Weekly Register-Call   111 Eureka Street, Central City, CO 80427

CHERRY HILLS
The Villager   8933 E. Union, Englewood, CO 80111

CHEYENNE WELLS
Range Ledger   141 S. First East, Cheyenne Wells, CO 80810

COLORADO CITY
Greenhorn Valley News   Fountain Square, P.O. Box 41, Colorado
                                    City, CO 81019

COLORADO SPRINGS
Black Forest News   112 N. Iowa., Ste 5, Colorado Springs, CO
                                    80909
Daily Transcript   22 N. Sierra Madre, Colorado Springs, CO
                                    80903
Gazette Telegraph   30 S. Prospect, Colorado Springs, CO 80903

COMMERCE CITY
Commerce City Express   7290 Magnolia, Commerce City, CO 80022

CONIFER
High Timber Times   26689 Pleasant Park Rd., Conifer, CO 80433

CORTEZ
Montezuma Valley Journal   37 E. Main, Cortez, CO 81321
Sentinel   37 E. Main, Cortez, CO 81321

CRAIG
Northwest Colorado Daily Press   466 Yampa Street, Craig, CO 81625

CREEDE
Mineral County Miner   7th & Main Street, Creede, CO 81130

CRESTED BUTTE
Crested Butte Chronicle & Pilot   500 Belleview, Crested Butte, CO 81224
Mountain Sun   508 Elk Ave., #3, Crested Butte, CO 81224

CRIPPLE CREEK
The Gold Rush   363 E. Bennett Ave., Cripple Creek, CO
                                    80814

DEER TRAIL
Tri-County Tribune   625 Second Avenue, Deer Trail, CO 80105

DEL NORTE
Del Norte Prospector   595 Columbia, Del Norte, CO 81132

DELTA
Delta County Independent   353 Main, Delta, CO 81416

DENVER
The Colorado Leader   3480 W. 1st Ave., Denver, CO 80219
The Colorado Statesman   1535 Grant St., Ste 280, Denver, CO 80203
The Daily Journal   101 University Blvd., Ste 260, Denver, CO
                                    80206
The Denver Business Journal   2401 15th St., Ste 350, Denver, Co 80202
The Denver Post   1560 Broadway, Denver, CO 80202
Denver Catholic Register   200 Josephine St., Denver, CO 80206
Herald-Dispatch   47 S. Federal Blvd., Denver, CO 80219
Intermountain Jewish News   1275 Sherman St., Ste 214, Denver, CO
                                    80203
La Voz Hispana de Colorado   812 Santa Fe Dr., Denver, CO 80204
Rocky Mountain Jiho   1255 19th St., Denver, CO 80202
Rocky Mountain News   400 W. Colfax, Denver, CO 80204
Westword   1621 18th Street, Ste 150, Denver, CO 80202

DOLORES
Dolores Star   211 Railroad, Dolores, CO 81323

DOVE CREEK
Dove Creek Press   390 N. Main, Dove Creek, CO 81324

DURANGO
Durango Herald   1275 Main, Durango, CO 81301

EADS
Kiowa County Press   1208 Maine, Eads, CO 81036

EAGLE
Eagle Valley Enterprise   011 Eagle Park East Dr., Eagle, CO 81631

EATON
North Weld Herald   206 First, Eaton, CO 80615

ENGLEWOOD
Englewood Sentinel   5801 W. 44th Ave., Unit L-1, Denver, CO
                                       80212

ESTES PARK
Estes Park Trail-Gazette   251 Moraine Ave., Estes Park, CO 80517

EVERGREEN
Canyon Courier   4009 Highway 74, Evergreen, CO 80439

FAIRPLAY
Park Co. Rep. & Fairplay Flume   56913 Highway 285, Bailey, CO 80421

FLAGLER
The Flagler News   317 Main Ave., Flagler, CO 80815

FLORENCE
Florence Citizen   204 S. Pikes Peak Ave., Florence, CO 81226

FORT COLLINS
The Coloradoan   1212 Riverside, Ft. Collins, CO 80525
Ft. Collins Triangle Review   530 S. College, Ft. Collins, CO 80524

FORT LUPTON
Ft. Lupton Press   515 4th Street, Ft. Lupton, CO 80642

FORT MORGAN
Fort Morgan Times   329 Main, Ft. Morgan, CO 80701

FOUNTAIN
El Paso County News   120 E. Ohio, Fountain, CO 80817

FOWLER
The Fowler Tribune   112 E. Cranston, Fowler, CO 81039

FREDERICK
Farmer & Miner   P.O. Box 400, Frederick, CO 80530

FRISCO
Summit Sentinel   40 W. Main, Frisco, CO 80443

FRUITA
The Fruita Times   136 E. Aspen, Fruita, CO 81521

GLENWOOD SPRINGS
Glenwood Post   2014 Grand Ave., Glenwood Springs, CO
                                       81601

GOLDEN
Golden Transcript · 1000 10th Street, Golden, CO 80401

GRANBY
Sky-Hi News · 242 E. Agate Ave., Granby, CO 80446

GRAND JUNCTION
The Daily Sentinel · 734 S. 7th St., Grand Junction, CO 81501

GREELEY
Greeley Tribune · 501 8th Ave., Greeley, CO 80631

GREENWOOD
The Villager · 8933 E. Union, Englewood, CO 80111

GUNNISON
Gunnison Country Times · 218 N. Wisconsin, Gunnison, CO 81230

HAXTUN
Haxtun Herald · 217 S. Colorado, Haxtun, CO 80731

HAYDEN
Hayden Valley Press · 466 Yampa Street, Craig, CO 81625

HOLYOKE
Holyoke Enterprise · 134 N. Interocean, Holyoke, CO 80734

HUGO
Eastern Colorado Plainsman · 329 4th St., Hugo, CO 80821

IDAHO SPRINGS
Clear Creek Courant · 1634 Miner St., Idaho Springs, CO 80452

JOHNSTOWN
Breeze · 7 S. Parish, Johnstown, CO 80534

JULESBURG
Julesburg Advocate · 100 Cedar St., Julesburg, CO 80737

KEENESBURG
Keene Valley Sun · 40 S. Main, Keenesburg, CO 80643
The New News · 40 S. Main, Keenesburg, CO 80643

KERSEY
The Voice · 326 1st Street, Kersey, Co 80644

KIOWA
Elbert County News · 308 Commanche, Kiowa, CO 80117

KREMMLING
Middle Park Times · 114 N. 3rd., Kremmling, CO 80459

LA JARA
Conejos County Citizen   517 Main, La Jara, CO 81140

LA JUNTA
Arkansas Valley Journal   7 W. 5th, La Junta, CO 81050
La Junta Tribune-Democrat   422 Colorado Ave., La Junta, CO 81050

LA SALLE
La Salle Leader   515 4th Street, Ft. Lupton, CO 80642

LA VETA
The Signature   303 Main, La Veta, CO 81055

LAFAYETTE
Lafayette News   111 N. Public Rd., Lafayette, CO 80026

LAKE CITY
Lake City Silver World   231 Silver St., Lake City, CO 81235

LAKEWOOD
Lakewood Sentinel   5801 W. 44th Ave., Unit L-1, Denver, CO
                                                80212
LAMAR
Lamar Daily News   310 S. 5th, Lamar, CO 81052

LAS ANIMAS
Bent County Democrat   516 Carson Ave., Las Animas, CO 81054

LEADVILLE
Herald Democrat   717 Harrison, Leadville, CO 80461

LIMON
The Limon Leader   809 Main, Limon, CO 80828

LITTLETON
Littleton Sentinel Independent   5801 W. 44th Ave., Unit L-1, Denver, CO
                                                80212
Littleton Times   5870 S. Curtice Street, Littleton, CO 80122

LONGMONT
Daily Times-Call   350 Terry St., Longmont, CO 80501

LOUISVILLE
Louisville Times   916 Main St., Louisville, CO 80027

LOVELAND
Daily Reporter-Herald   450 N. Cleveland, Loveland, CO 80537

LYONS
The Old Lyons Recorder   430 Main St., Lyons, CO 80540

MANCOS
Mancos Times Tribune   135 W. Grand, Mancos, CO 81328

MANITOU SPRINGS
Pikes Peak Journal   22 Ruxton Ave., Manitou Springs, CO 80829

MEEKER
Meeker Herald   4th & Main, Meeker, CO 81641

MONTE VISTA
The Monte Vista Journal   229 Adams, Monte Vista, CO 81144

MONTROSE
Daily Press   535 S. First, Montrose, CO 81401

MONUMENT
Tribune   283 Washington, Monument, CO 80132

NEDERLAND
Mountain-Ear   20 Lakeview Drive, #208, Nederland, CO
                                         80466

NORTHGLENN
Northglenn/Thornton Sentinel   5801 W. 44th Ave., Unit L-1, Denver, CO
                                         80212

NUCLA
San Miguel Basin Forum   807 Main St., Nucla, CO 81424

ORDWAY
The Ordway New Era   223 Main, Ordway, CO 81063

OURAY
Ouray County Plaindealer   333 6th Ave., Ouray, CO 81427

PAGOSA SPRINGS
Pagosa Springs Sun   466 Pagosa St., Pagosa Springs, CO 81147

PALISADE
The Palisade Tribune and   124 W. 3rd., Palisade, CO 81526
  Valley Report

PARKER
The Parker Trail   10521 S. Parker Road, Parker, CO 80134

PLATTEVILLE
Platteville Herald   515 4th, Platteville, CO 80642

PUEBLO
The Colorado Tribune   447 Park Dr., Pueblo, CO 81005
The Pueblo Chieftain   825 W. 6th St., Pueblo, CO 81003

RANGLEY
The Rangley Times   713 E. Main St., Rangely, CO 81648

RIFLE
Citizen Telegram   123 E. 3rd., Rifle, CO 81650

ROCKY FORD
Daily Gazette   912 Elm, Rocky Ford, CO 81067

SAGUACHE
Saguache Crescent   316 4th., Saguache, CO 81149

SALIDA
The Mountain Mail   125 E. 2nd, Salida, CO 81201

SAN LUIS
Costilla County Free Press   120 Main Street, San Luis, CO 81152

SILVERTON
The Silverton Standard   1257 Greene St., Silverton, CO 81433
 & The Miner

SIMLA
Ranchland News   115 Sioux Ave., Simla, CO 80835

SNOWMASS VILLAGE
Snowmass Sun   16 Kearns Rd. #211, Snowmass Village, CO
                                 81615

SOUTH FORK
South Fork Times   29411 W. U.S. 160, South Fork, CO 81154

SPRINGFIELD
Plainsman Herald   849 Main, Springfield, CO 81073

STEAMBOAT SPRINGS
Steamboat Pilot   1041 Lincoln, Steamboat Springs, Co 80477

STERLING
Journal-Advocate   504 N. 3rd., Sterling, CO 80751

STRASBURG
Eastern Colorado News   1522 Main St., Strasburg, CO 80136

STRATTON
Stratton Spotlight   125 Colorado Ave., Stratton, CO 80836

TELLURIDE
Telluride Times-Journal   232 W. Colorado, Telluride, CO 81435

THORNTON
Thornton/Northglen Sentinel 5801 W. 44th Ave. Unit L-1, Denver, CO 80212

TRINIDAD
Chronicle-News 200 W. Church, Trinidad, CO 81082

VAIL
The Vail Trail 164 Railroad, Suite 150, Minturn, CO 81645

WALDEN
Jackson County Star 417 5th St., Walden, CO 80480

WALSENBURG
Huerfano World 111 W. 7th St., Walsenburg, CO 81089

WESTCLIFFE
Wet Mountain Tribune 404 Main, Westcliffe, CO 81252

WESTMINSTER
Westminster Sentinel 5801 W. 44th Ave., Unit L-1, Denver, CO 80212
Westminster Window 7380 Lowell Blvd., Westminster, CO 80030

WHEAT RIDGE
Wheat Ridge Sentinel 5801 W. 44th Ave., Unit L-1, Denver, CO 80212

WIGGINS
Wiggins Courier 213 Dickson, Wiggins, CO 80654

WINDSOR
The Windsor Beacon 425 Main, Windsor, CO 80550

WINTER PARK
Winter Park Manifest 78622 Winter Park Dr., Winter Park, CO 80482

WOODLAND PARK
Ute Pass Courier 1200 E. Highway 24, Woodland Park, CO 80866

WRAY
Wray Gazette 411 Main, Wray, CO 80758

YUMA
Yuma Pioneer 207 S. Main, Yuma, CO 80759

Source: Colorado Press Association.

Appendix CC

COLORADO STATE SENATORS

County	Senator	District	Phone (all 303)
Adams	Johansen, Jean	24	866-4865
	Martinez, Bob	25	866-4865
	Strickland, Ted	23	866-3342
Alamosa	Pastore, Bob	5	866-4853
Arapahoe	Considine, Terry	26	866-4866
	Fenlon, Jack	28	866-4866
	Mutzebaugh, Dick	29	866-4866
	Owens, Bill	27	866-4866
	Pascoe, Pat	34	866-4865
	Wham, Dottie	35	866-4866
Archuletta	Cassidy, Sam	6	866-4865
Baca	Rizzuto, Jim	2	866-4865
Bent	Rizzuto, Jim	2	866-4865
Boulder	Hopper, Sally	13	866-4866
	Hume, Sandy	17	866-4866
	Mendez, Jana	18	866-4865
Chaffee	Pastore, Bob	5	866-4853
Cheyenne	Rizzuto, Jim	2	866-4865
Clear Creek	Hopper, Sally	13	866-4866
Conejos	Pastore, Bob	5	866-4853
Costilla	Pastore, Bob	5	866-4853
Crowley	Rizzuto, Jim	2	866-4855
Custer	McCormick, Harold	4	871-0724
Delta	Cassidy, Sam	6	866-4865
	Pastore, Bob	5	866-4853

Denver	Gallagher, Dennis	30	866-4865
	Groff, Regis	33	866-4865
	Pascoe, Pat	34	866-4865
	Peterson, Ray	32	866-4865
	Sandovol, Donald	31	866-4861
	Wham, Dottie	35	866-4866
Dolores	Cassidy, Sam	6	866-4865
Douglas	Mutzebaugh, Dick	29	866-4866
Eagle	Hopper, Sally	13	866-4866
Elbert	Bird, Mike	9	866-4866
El Paso	Bird, Mike	9	866-4866
	Powers, Ray	10	866-4866
	Tebedo, MaryAnne	12	866-4866
	Wells, Jeffrey	11	866-3341
Fremont	McCormick, Harold	4	866-4866
Garfield	Wattenberg, Dave	8	866-4866
Gilpin	Hopper, Sally	13	866-4866
Grand	Wattenberg, Dave	8	866-4866
Gunnison	Pastore, Bob	5	866-4853
Hinsdale	Pastore, Bob	5	866-4853
Huerfano	Rizzuto, Jim	2	866-4865
Jackson	Wattenberg, Dave	8	866-4866
Jefferson	Allison, Bonnie	21	866-4866
	Hopper, Sally	13	866-4866
	Meiklejohn, Al	19	866-4866
	Mutzebaugh, Dick	29	866-4866
	Peterson, Ray	32	866-4565
	Schroeder, Bill	22	866-4866
	Traylor, Claire	20	866-4866
Kiowa	Rizzuto, Jim	2	866-4865
Kit Carson	Ament, Don	1	866-4866
Lake	McCormick, Harold	4	866-4866
La Plata	Cassidy, Sam	6	866-4865
Larimer	Roberts, Jim	15	866-4866
	Schaffer, Bob	14	866-4865
	Wattenberg, Dave	8	866-4866
Las Animas	Rizzuto, Jim	2	866-4865
Lincoln	Powers Ray	10	866-4866
Logan	Ament, Don	1	866-4866
Mesa	Bishop, Tillie	7	866-4866
Mineral	Pastore, Bob	5	866-4853
Moffat	Wattenberg, Dave	8	866-4866
Montezuma	Cassidy, Sam	6	866-4865
Montrose	Cassidy, Sam	6	866-4865

Morgan	Ament, Don	1	866-4866
Otero	Rizzuto, Jim	2	866-4865
Ouray	Cassidy, Sam	6	866-4865
Park	McCormick, Harold	4	866-4866
Phillips	Ament, Don	1	866-4866
Pitkin	Hopper, Sally	13	866-4866
Prowers	Rizzuto, Jim	2	866-4865
Pueblo	McCormick, Harold	4	866-4866
	Rizzuto, James	2	866-4865
	Trujillo, Sr., Larry	3	866-2318
Rio Blanco	Wattenberg, Dave	8	866-4866
Rio Grande	Pastore, Bob	5	866-4853
Routt	Wattenberg, Dave	8	866-4866
Saguache	Pastore, Bob	5	866-4853
San Juan	Cassidy, Sam	6	866-4866
San Miguel	Cassidy, Sam	6	866-4866
Sedgwick	Ament, Don	1	866-4866
Summit	Hopper, Sally	13	866-4866
Teller	Tebedo, MaryAnne	12	866-4866
Washington	Ament, Don	1	866-4866
Weld	Ament, Don	1	866-4866
	Roberts, Jim	16	866-4866
Yuma	Ament, Don	1	866-4866

Appendix DD

COLORADO STATE HOUSE REPRESENTATIVES

County	Representative	District	Phone (all 303)
Adams	DeHerrera, Guillermo	30	866-2931
	Fleming, Faye	31	866-2918
	Jones, Matt	34	866-2910
	June, Vi	35	866-2843
	Moellenberg, R.D.	64	866-2940
	Reeser, Jeannie	32	866-2964
	Snyder, Carol	33	866-4667
Alamosa	Entz, Lewis	60	866-2963
Arapahoe	Adkins, Jeanne	40	866-2936
	Blickensderfer, Tom	37	866-2951
	Coffman, Mike	49	866-2944
	Grant, Patrick	9	866-2938
	Kerns, Peggy	62	866-2919
	Moellenberg, R.D.	64	866-2940
	Neale, Betty	10	866-2937
	Pankey, Phil	38	866-2953
	Ruddick, Steve	36	866-5522
	Schauer, Paul	39	866-2935
	Shoemaker, Jeff	11	866-5510
Archuleta	Dyer, Jim	59	866-2914
Baca	Young, Brad	63	866-3911
Bent	Young, Brad	63	866-3911

Boulder	Flemimg, Faye	31	866-2918
	Johnson, Stan	13	866-2942
	Rupert, Dorothy	14	866-2915
	Swenson, Betty	12	866-2945
	Wright, Ruth	15	866-5523
Chaffee	Chlouber, Ken	61	866-2952
Cheyenne	Moelleberg, R.D.	64	866-2940
Clear Creek	Williams, Sam	53	866-2920
Conejos	Entz, Lewis	60	866-2963
Costilla	Entz, Lewis	60	866-2963
Crowley	Young, Brad	63	866-3911
Custer	Chlouber, Ken	61	866-2952
Delta	Acquafresca, Steve	58	866-2955
	Foster, Tim	54	866-5525
Denver	DeHerrera, Guillermo	30	866-2931
	Faatz, Jeanne	1	866-2966
	Grant, Patrick	9	866-2938
	Hernandez, Phillip	5	866-2925
	Hernandez, Tony	2	866-2911
	Knox, Wayne	3	866-2921
	Kopel, Jerry	6	866-2916
	Mares, Donald J.	4	866-2954
	Moellenberg, R.D.	64	866-2940
	Neale, Betty	10	866-2937
	Shoemaker, Jeff	11	866-5510
	Tanner Gloria	7	866-2909
	Webb, Wilma	8	866-5524
Dolores	Acquafresca, Steve	58	866-2955
Douglas	Adkins, Jeanne	40	866-2936
Eagle	McInnis, Scott	57	866-2348
	Williams, Dan	56	866-2962
Elbert	Adkins, Jeanne M.	40	866-2936
	Moellenberg, R.D.	64	866-2940
El Paso	Berry, Charles E.	21	866-2349
	Duke, Charles	20	866-2924
	Epps, Mary Ellen	19	866-2946
	Fagan, Renny	22	866-2912
	Greenwood, Daphne	17	866-3069
	Martin, Bill	16	866-2965
	Ratterree, Tom	18	866-2960
Fremont	Arveschoug, Steve	44	866-2949
	Chlouber, Ken	61	866-2952
Garfield	McInnis, Scott	57	866-2348
Gilpin	Williams, Samuel	53	866-2920

Grand	Williams, Dan	56	866-2962
Gunnison	Chlouber, Ken	61	866-2952
	Entz, Lewis	60	866-2963
Hinsdale	Entz, Lewis	60	866-2963
Huerfano	Salas, Mike	43	866-2948
Jackson	Williams, Dan	56	866-2962
Jefferson	Agler, Vickie	28	866-2939
	Anderson, Norma	52	866-2927
	Faatz, Jeanne	1	866-2966
	Fish, Marleen	23	866-2967
	Grampsas, Tony	25	866-2957
	Killian, Pat	24	866-2956
	Lawrence, Michelle	29	866-2950
	Miller, Pat	27	866-3540
	Tucker, Shirleen	26	866-2923
	Williams, Sam	53	866-2920
Kiowa	Young, Brad	63	866-3911
Kit Carson	Moellenberg, R.D.	64	866-2940
Lake	Chlouber, Ken	61	866-2952
La Plata	Dyer, Jim	59	866-2914
Larimer	Irwin, John	45	866-2947
	Owen, David	48	866-2943
	Redder, Thomas	46	866-4569
	Reeves, Peggy	47	866-2917
Las Animas	Salas, Mike	43	866-2948
Lincoln	Moellenberg, R.D.	64	866-2940
Logan	Eisenach, Robert	65	866-3706
Mesa	Foster, Tim	54	866-5525
	Prinster, Dan	55	866-2908
Mineral	Entz, Lewis	60	866-2963
Moffat	Williams, Dan	56	866-2962
Montezuma	Acquafresca, Steve	58	866-2955
	Dyer, Jim	59	866-2914
Montrose	Acquafresca, Steve	58	866-2955
Morgan	Eisenach, Robert	65	866-3706
Otero	Salas, Mike	43	866-2939
	Young Brad	63	866-3911
Ouray	Acquafresca, Steve	58	866-2955
Park	Chlouber, Ken	61	866-2952
Phillips	Moellenberg, R.D.	64	866-2940
Pitkin	McInnis, Scott	57	866-2348
Prowers	Young, Brad	63	866-3911

Pueblo	Arveschoug, Steve	44	866-2949
	Romero, Gilbert	42	866-2968
	Salas, Mike	43	866-2948
	Thiebaut, Jr., Bill	41	866-2922
Rio Blanco	McInnis, Scott	57	866-2348
Rio Grande	Entz, Lewis H.	60	866-2963
Routt	Williams, Dan	56	866-2962
Saguache	Entz, Lewis	60	866-2963
San Juan	Dyer, Jim	59	866-2914
San Miguel	Acquafresca, Steve	58	866-2955
Sedgwick	Eisenach, Robert	65	866-3706
Summit	Williams, Sam	53	866-2920
Teller	Chlouber, Ken	61	866-2952
Washington	Moellenberg, R.D.	64	866-2940
Weld	Fleming, Faye	31	866-2918
	Jerke, William	51	866-2907
	Owen, David T.	48	866-2943
	Bont, Dick	50	866-2929
Yuma	Moellenberg, R.D.	64	866-2940

GLOSSARY

A

Appraisal—the dollar value assigned to a property by the county assessor; it is *not* the property's current fair market value. Also referred to as "assessor's appraisal," "total actual value," "actual value," "appraised value," and "assessor's value."

Appraisal card—the assessor's written inventory of information about a piece of property, usually including land size and contour, square feet of buildings, number of baths, etc.

Arbitration—the non-judicial submission of a controversy to selected third parties for their determination.

Arm's-length transaction—a transaction involving two parties who are unrelated to one another, and whose mutual dealings with each other are influenced only by the independence of each.

Assessment—an official valuation of real property for tax purposes, based on appraisals. Multiplying the appraisal value by the *assessment rate* determines the assessment.

Assessment rate—the percentage of a property's total value used to calculate a property's assessed value (assessment). Currently, the assessment rate is 14.34 percent for residential properties and 29 percent for commercial properties.

Assessor's appraisal—see "Appraisal"
Assessor's value—see "Appraisal"

B

Base period—the time period used in calculating appraisals; the period of property sale dates that each county
assessor uses in collecting data to determine property
values. Example: January 1, 1989—June 30, 1990.
Board of Assessment Appeals—a state agency set up to
allow a taxpayer to seek relief from the county Board of
Equalization's opinion of value (decision rendered in the
second round of protest); the third round of protest.
Board of Equalization—the county reviewing agency
holding the authority to adjust inequities in property assessments. The Board is overseen by county commissioners and usually operated by the county attorney's office
for the purpose of listening to taxpayer appeals of the
county assessor's valuation on property; the second round
of protest.

C

Capitalization rate—the rate of return that an investor
wants on his/her cash outlay; calculated to include the
purchase price and closing costs in a cash transaction.
Comparables—sold properties that are similar to a particular property being evaluated and are used to indicate a
reasonable fair market value for the subject property.
Cost approach—an approach to the evaluation of property
based on the property's reproduction cost; generally, the
current reproduction cost of a building, minus depreciation
plus the value of the land.
Court of Appeals—a court possessing jurisdiction to review the law as applied to a prior determination of the
same case (fourth round of protest).

D

Denial notice—a negative answer to a taxpayer's protest.
Depreciation—a loss in value due to any cause; any condition that adversely affects the value of an improvement.

E

Equalization—the adjustment of the appraised valuation of real property to achieve a parity with the level of appraisal of other similar properties, without regard to the properties' true value.

Expert witness—a person having special knowledge of a subject about which he/she is to testify.

F

Foreclosure—selling of property to the general public in order to satisfy a debt.

G

Goodwill—an intangible asset arising from the reputation of a business; the expectation of continued public patronage; including other intangible assets such as trade name, relationship within the community, supplier relations, etc.

H

Hearing—a conference, meeting, or proceeding wherein evidence is taken for the purpose of determining an issue and reaching a decision based on that evidence.

Hearing officer—the individual(s) who have been granted authority to make recommendations to the county commissioners as a result of information gained at a hearing.

I

Improvements—valuable additions made to property which amount to more than repairs, costing labor and money, and are intended to enhance the value of property.

Income approach—an approach to the valuation or appraisal of real property as determined by the amount of net income the property will produce over its remaining economic life.

L

Land valuation—that value applied to land as determined by the assessor as if the land were vacant.

M

Market approach—an approach to the valuation or appraisal of real property based on the principle of comparison; comparing sale prices of similar properties which were sold.

Mass appraisal method—the computer-assisted method of appraising large numbers of properties.

Mill levy—one-tenth of a cent (.001); multiplied by the assessment to determine property taxes.

N

Neighborhood adjustment (NHAJ)—a technical term having the purpose of adjusting the difference in value of one similar neighborhood to another. In reality, it is often utilized for the purpose of making the results of two different appraisal methods (cost and market) on the same property the same.

Notice of valuation—a statement offering the assessor's opinion of the total actual value of a piece of property.

O

Official appraisal date—the day and year selected for tax purposes to establish a property's value as of that moment in time.

P

Personal property—items which are real and often movable; property which is not classified as real property.

Petition for Abatement or Refund of Taxes Form—form used for the purpose of seeking relief or refund of property taxes.

Property identification number—the number used by the

assessor to identify a specific piece of property. Often referred to as "schedule number."

R

Real property—the earth's surface, the air above, and the ground below, as well as almost all attachments to the land, including buildings, structures, fixtures, fences, and improvements erected upon or affixed to the same.

Real Property Transfer Declaration Form—form used to convey information to the assessor about the purchase a buyer has made.

Reappraisal—a new determination of value, based on a new date of value.

Reappraisal date—see "Official appraisal date"

Request to Combine Property Form—form used to combine separately taxed pieces of property.

Residential property—single-family houses, duplexes, triplexes, apartment buildings, and mobile homes.

S

Sales ratio analysis—a list of properties sold within a base period for the purpose of comparing the assessor's value with the actual sale price in that same time period.

Stipulation—an agreement, admission, or concession made by all parties for valuation purposes; enforceable only for said year.

T

Taxing district—the geographic location or boundaries in which a tax can be imposed on property.

Total actual value—See "Appraisal"

V

Valuation—see "Appraisal"

INDEX

BIOGRAPHY

Ed C. Tomlinson, a Realtor for 20 years, is a broker/associate with RE/MAX West in Arvada. He has been researching the state's property tax assessment system for over 10 years, and is recognized throughout Colorado as an expert in the field.

His working knowledge of the system is based on thorough study of assessors' policy and procedure manuals, training with appraisers from assessors' offices, years of experience with the property tax protest procedure. He has conducted hundreds of protests, and has been featured extensively by broadcast and print media on the subjects of property tax assessment and the status of the Colorado real estate market. He has also been invited to speak before the Colorado Senate and House Interim Tax Committee to offer recommendations on improving Colorado's property tax system.

He is a Certified Senior Appraiser with the National Association of Real Estate Appraisers and is a senior arbitrator for the Better Business Bureau. He is a member of the Colorado Real Estate Educators Association, the National Association of Realtors, the Colorado Association of Realtors, the Colorado Public Expenditures Council, the Apartment Association of Metro Denver, the National Apartment Association, and the Northwest Metro Chamber of Commerce.

Tomlinson also serves as Director and Treasurer for the Jefferson County Board of Realtors, and as a Director for the Colorado Association of Realtors and the North Jeffco Park and Recreation Foundation.

DISCOVER HOW TO ESCAPE EXCESSIVE PROPERTY TAX ASSESSMENTS!

ORDER FORM

YES, I want ____ copies of *Overtaxed!* at $8.95 each, plus $2 shipping per book. (Colorado residents please include 28 cents state sales tax.) Allow 10 days for delivery.

Name _____ Phone _____

Address _____

City/State/Zip _____

Card # _____ Expires _____

Signature _____

☐ Check/MO enclosed • Charge my ☐ VISA ☐ MasterCard

Check your leading bookstore or
call in your credit card order to: 303-424-5656

Please make your check payable and return to:

Diamond Publications
5440 Ward Road, Suite 110
Arvada, CO 80002